cool craft

Published by Vivays Publishing
www.vivays-publishing.com

A catalogue record for this book is
available from the British Library

ISBN 978-1-908126-11-5

Publishing Director: Lee Ripley
Design: Struktur Design

Printed in China

cool craft

Bridget Bodoano

Vivays Publishing

Knitting

Sewing

Stitching

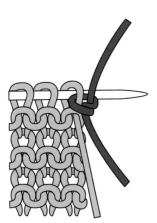

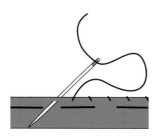

Contents

Accessories

Paper

Design & Technology

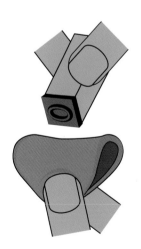

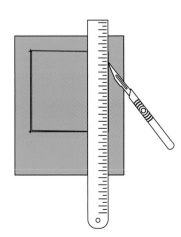

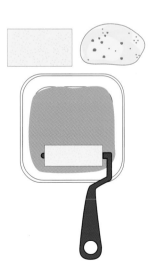

cool craft

Bridget Bodoano

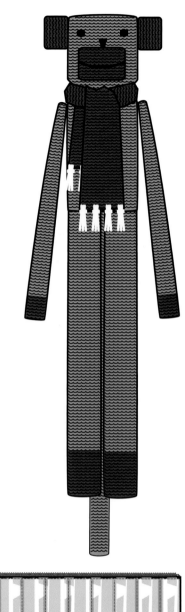

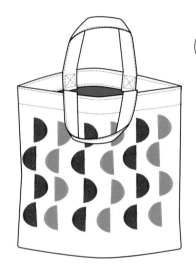

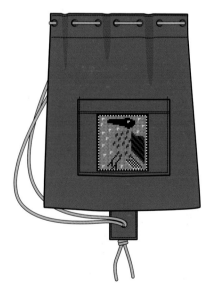

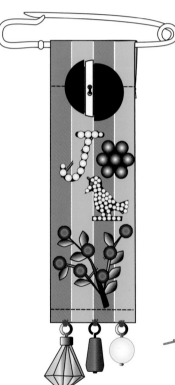

Craft is back and people of all ages are discovering – or re-discovering – the joys of making something by hand. Not only is it a great antidote to conspicuous consumerism it also gives you something to do while winding down, gossiping, watching TV or listening to your favourite music.

There are lots of shops selling craft materials and artists; supplies, and the internet offers a vast range of both materials and instructions. A lot of the projects on offer are a bit fussy and while the process of making is enjoyable the end result is not necessarily something that anyone would wish their friends to see. This book aims to lure style-conscious people into craft with the promise of things to make that they can be proud of and happy to wear or use.

The basic projects in the *knitting* and *sewing* sections are deliberately simple with no fancy shapes, awkward corners, gussets or trims to deter the beginner. Most of the designs are based on rectangles and straight lines. Not only does this make them easier to make it gives the projects a crisp, contemporary feel and keeping it simple also means that it is easier to achieve a good finish.

Instructions are given for basic techniques which will enable you to make simple items, but these basics are all you need to make the more adventurous projects in *stitching* and *accessories*.

The projects in the *paper* chapter include opportunities to make use of photography and technology as well as your artistic talents to create your own books, new ways of displaying photographs and to make grown-up versions of collage and cut-outs.

The section on *design and technology* outlines how digital cameras, printers and ever-more sophisticated computer programmes can be used along with materials for making your own prints and transfers to make quite sophisticated and high quality stuff that is unique to you.

Templates and charts are included for you to use but it is hoped that you will be inspired to create your own designs and patterns.

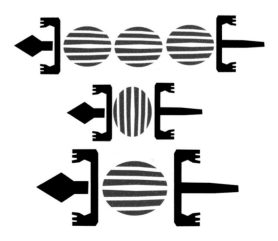

Knitting

Learn to knit, purl, cast on and cast off and you can produce accessories that won't disgrace your designer outfits or ruin your credibility.

Knitting

Once an activity which took place mainly in the privacy of your own home, knitters have come out of the closet and can now be seen on buses, in cafes and even in special cinema screenings where they leave the lights up so you won't drop a stitch.

Knitting wools have also escaped from fusty, dusty shops to show themselves off in buzzy boutiques and even glamorous department stores. And if knitting puts you in mind of itchy, ill-fitting jumpers or complicated shapes and stitches you may be surprised that simply by learning to knit, purl, cast on and cast off you can produce accessories that won't disgrace your designer outfits or ruin your credibility.

Getting started

Materials

Knitting yarns come in a variety of thicknesses and types of materials. Wool is the traditional fibre, but there are lots of synthetics and wool/synthetic mixes as well as cotton and metallic threads.

Knitting needles (sometimes called pins) come in a range of thicknesses to suit different thicknesses of yarn. The label normally tells you what size needles to use. If you are following a specific pattern where measurements are vital you should use the recommended size, but for simple projects such as bags and scarves you can experiment using smaller needles for a denser fabric or larger needles to give a looser, lacier look. If you use thin yarns on thin needles your knitting will grow slowly, so for quicker results go for chunky yarn and chunky needles.

Getting started

If you are a beginner it's a good idea to do some practice runs before embarking on a project. Begin by casting on around 20 stitches, start knitting and keep going. It may look a mess to begin with but it gets easier. Keep the yarn taut but don't hold it too tightly, and don't wind it too tightly around the needles. Keep control of the yarn by looping it over your index finger and for extra control hook it round your little finger.

tip:

Advice for the beginner

Good knitting yarns are expensive so buy some cheap yarn to practise with.

Avoid yarns that are too thick, too thin or too 'fancy' as they can be difficult to work with.

Chunky and multi-coloured yarns will cover up minor mistakes, imperfections and uneven tensions.

Materials

Getting started

Casting on – Loop method

This is the easiest and most basic method of casting on.

1: Wind the wool round your thumb leaving a long tail.

2: Push the needle through and slip the loop off your thumb and on to the needle.

3: Wind the wool around your thumb again and make the next loop as before.

4: Repeat until you have the number of stitches you need.

tip:

Keep the stitches evenly spaced as you go, if you don't you could end up with an uneven bottom edge

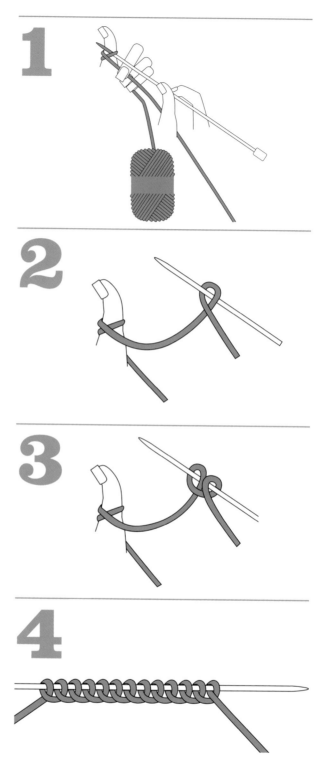

Casting off

Start casting off at the beginning of a row. When you have two stitches on the right-hand needle (1) use the left-hand needle to loop the first stitch (2) and pull it over over the last stitch (3). Knit the next stitch and repeat the process until just one stitch remains. Cut off the yarn (leaving a long tail), thread the end of it through the last stitch (4) and gently pull it tight.

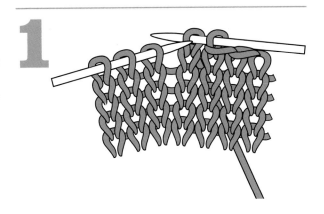

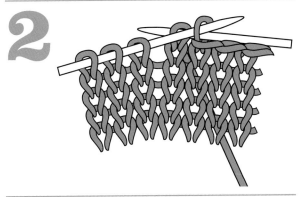

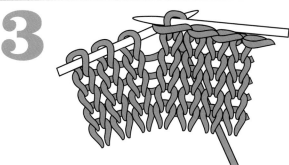

tip:

Edges can end up wobbly and uneven but you can keep them neat by slipping the first stitch of every row and knitting the last stitch (even if that stitch would normally be a purl).

A slip stitch is a stitch that is slipped off the needle without winding the wool round.

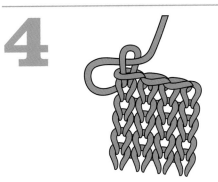

Casting off

The knit stitch

1: With the yarn at the back of the work push the right-hand knitting needle from left to right through the front of the first stitch on the left-hand needle. Wind the yarn anti-clockwise round the tip of the right-hand needle and behind the left-hand needle.

2: Use the tip of the right-hand needle to pull this yarn through the stitch to form a loop on the right-hand needle.

3: Slide the old stitch off the end of the left-hand needle.

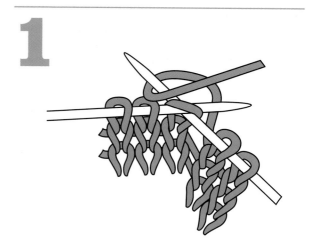

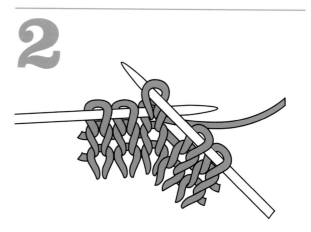

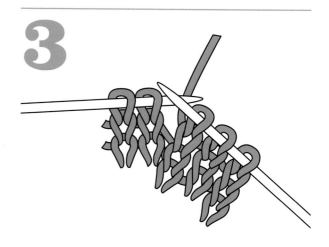

The purl stitch

1: With the yarn at the front of the work push the right-hand needle from right to left through the front of the first stitch on the left-hand needle.
2: Wind the yarn anti-clockwise round the tip of the right-hand needle.
3: Use the tip of the right-hand needle to pull this yarn through the stitch to form a loop on the right-hand needle. Slide the old stitch off the end of the left-hand needle.

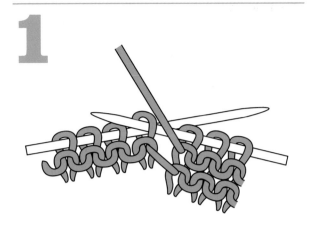

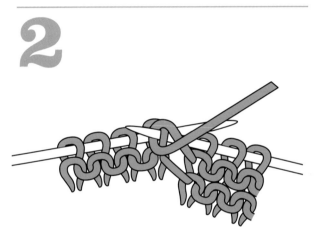

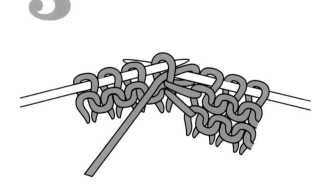

The purl stitch

Simple stitches

When you knit a stitch the bar made by the yarn is on the back, when you purl the bar is on the front. This is how different patterns are created. There are some very fancy knitting stitches that require equally fancy techniques and instructions, but you can make create quite a few effects using the smooth appearance of knit and the bobbliness of purl.

In pattern instructions K means knit the stitch and P means purl it. The number following denotes how many stitches.

Garter stitch

If you knit every row you end up with 'garter stitch' which is a mixture of the bobbly and the smooth. It is not a very dense stitch and it is quite stretchy.

Stocking stitch

This is formed by one knit row followed by one purl row to give a smooth, close, flat stitch on one side and a dense, bobbly finish on the other. The knit side (stocking stitch) is normally used as the front but sometimes the purl side (reverse stocking stitch) is used as it gives a textured look and is denser than garter stitch.

Rib

Knitting one stitch and purling the next (K1 P1) for the whole row and knitting into the knit stitch and purling into the purl on the second row forms a stretchy 'rib' or 'welt' which you will find round the bottom and the cuffs of knitwear.

Moss stitch

K1 P1 as in rib but on every second row you knit into the purl and purl into the knit. This results in an even, textured look which is quite dense, holds its shape well and doesn't curl at the edges.

Box stitch

This is a bigger form of moss stitch with the knit and purl stitches workded in multiples of two or more. An easy way to get a chunky, distinctive look.

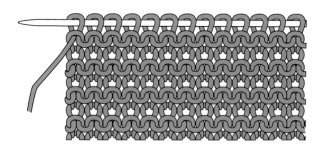

Garter stitch

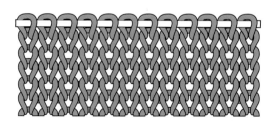

Stocking stitch (front)

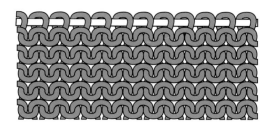

Stocking stitch (back)

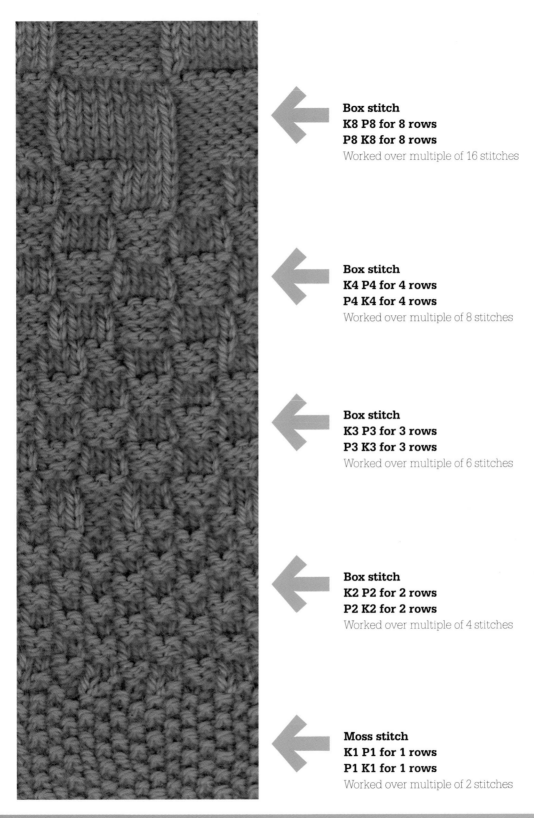

Box stitch
K8 P8 for 8 rows
P8 K8 for 8 rows
Worked over multiple of 16 stitches

Box stitch
K4 P4 for 4 rows
P4 K4 for 4 rows
Worked over multiple of 8 stitches

Box stitch
K3 P3 for 3 rows
P3 K3 for 3 rows
Worked over multiple of 6 stitches

Box stitch
K2 P2 for 2 rows
P2 K2 for 2 rows
Worked over multiple of 4 stitches

Moss stitch
K1 P1 for 1 rows
P1 K1 for 1 rows
Worked over multiple of 2 stitches

Moss stitch and Box stitch

Project: 01
Scarves

The easiest thing to knit is a scarf. Just cast on some stitches and keep going. A long scarf will require a lot of yarn so if you are using an expensive yarn be prepared for the high cost or choose short length. If you are impatient and only have a small amount of wool, knit a skinny tie.

How big and how many stitches?

The projects in this book are all based on rectangles and the choice of needle size and the thickness of yarn is left to you. The measurements are also up to you though suggested dimensions are included with the projects. The main thing you need to know is how many stitches to cast on and this is easy to work out.

The number of stitches needed for a specified width depends on the thickness of the yarn, the needle size and your own style of knitting. Some people knit more loosely than others. The number of stitches per centimetre or inch will vary according to your own technique. By knitting up a sample you can work out the number of stitches and rows required to produce a specified dimension.

This sample also allows you to assess whether you want a closer, tighter finish, in which case use smaller needles or a thicker yarn, or if you want a looser feel, in which case you could try larger needles or a thinner yarn.

Cast on 30 stitches and knit at least 15 rows. Lay the knitting out flat. Place a ruler over the middle of the work and count how many stitches there are in a specified area. For example, if 10 of your stitches measure 8 centimetres you will need 30 stitches for a scarf 24 centimetres wide. If there are 4 of your stitches per inch then you will need 40 stitches for a scarf 10 inches wide.

tip:

To make calculations easier count stitches in multiples that divide easily into the required measurement. For example for something 12 cm or 12 inches wide count the stitches in twelves or fours.

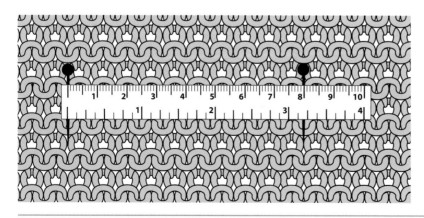

Short scarf
Suggested size for short scarf
120 x 24 cm (47 x 9 ½ in).

Long scarves
Suggested size for long scarf
180 x 24 cm (72 x 9½ in).

Skinny tie
Suggested size for skinny tie
120 x 4 cm (47 x 1½ in).

tip:

Stripes are nice but you end up with lots of ends to sew in which can make the edges untidy and lumpy. If you want stripes make them very wide.

tip:

For scarves and ties avoid using stocking stitch (one row knit and one row purl) as it tends to curl in at the edges and has an obvious front and back. Stick to garter stitch, or moss or box stitch.

Project: 02
Hats

These simple hats are made from folded rectangles and only require a small amount of sewing. Dress them up with jewellery, tassels or pom-poms. Garter stitch is the easiest but as the sides are sewn up you can also use stocking stitch. If you want something textured use moss or box stitch.

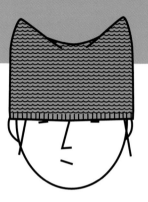 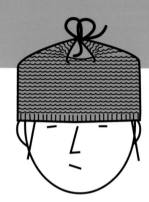

Use a ready-made woolly hat to work out the measurements needed and then work out your tension and the number of stitches and rows as shown on page 18.

Version 1
Making the hat from a wide rectangle rather than a long length means that the seams are at the back and on top rather than at the sides where they would be more noticeable.

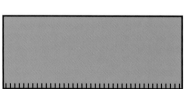 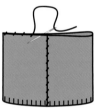 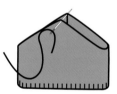

1
Knit the rectangle to your preferred dimensions.

2
Join ends to make a tube and sew up along the back seam.

3
Sew up along the top seam.

4
Turn right side out and wear ...

5
... or fold it in half and join the two points together.

tip:

For a snug fit knit 6 rows of K1 P1 rib at the beginning of version 1 and at both ends for version 2.

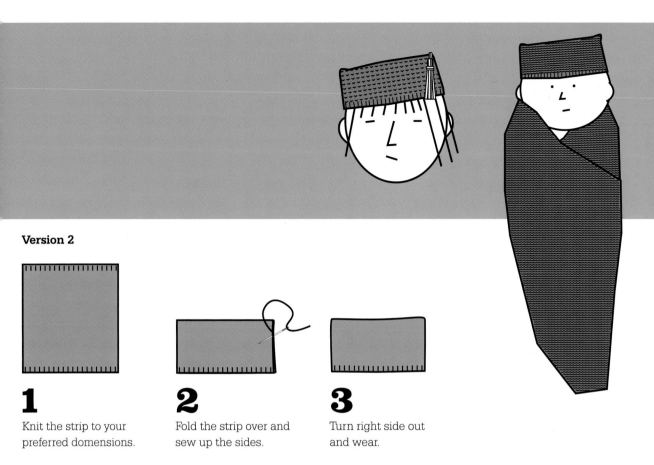

Version 2

1
Knit the strip to your preferred domensions.

2
Fold the strip over and sew up the sides.

3
Turn right side out and wear.

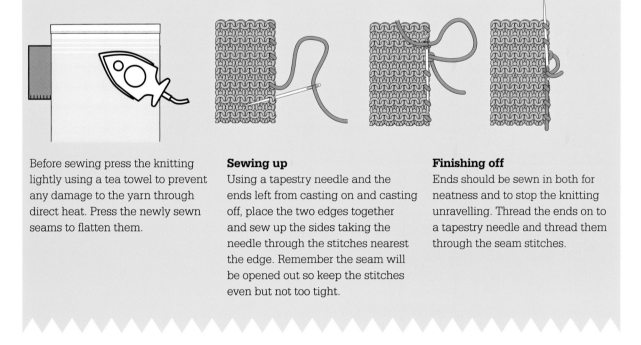

Before sewing press the knitting lightly using a tea towel to prevent any damage to the yarn through direct heat. Press the newly sewn seams to flatten them.

Sewing up
Using a tapestry needle and the ends left from casting on and casting off, place the two edges together and sew up the sides taking the needle through the stitches nearest the edge. Remember the seam will be opened out so keep the stitches even but not too tight.

Finishing off
Ends should be sewn in both for neatness and to stop the knitting unravelling. Thread the ends on to a tapestry needle and thread them through the seam stitches.

Project: 03
Bags

Turn a hat upside down, sew on some handles and you've got a bag.

Knitted fabrics are quite stretchy so in order to ensure bags are up to the job make the knitting quite dense and close. Use smaller needles and choose a tightly spun, robust yarns.

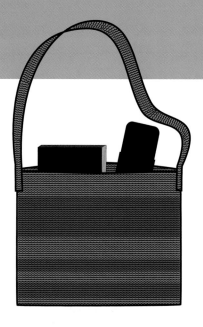

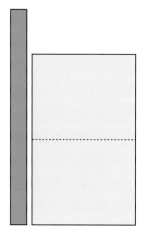

Version 1

For a bag measuring 25 cm wide and 20 cm deep (10 x 8 in) with a handle 4 cm wide and 70 cm long (1½ x 28 in).

tip:

Knit the handle on smaller needles. This will make it stronger and less stretchy.

1

Knit two pieces:
1 x 40 x 25 cm
(15¾ x 10 in)
1 x 4cm (1½ in)
x 70cm (28 in).

2

Press lightly.
Fold the larger piece in half lengthways and sew up the sides.

3

Turn right side out. Pin the long handle piece across the side seam allowing 8 cm (3 in) overlap. Sew on the handle using the same coloured yarn and small, neat stitches on the outside. Add extra stitches on the inside at the top for strength.

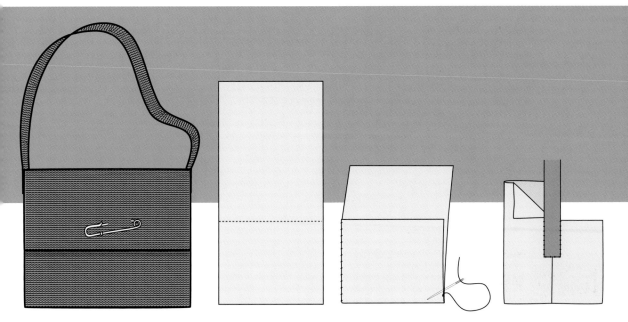

Version 2

For a bag measuring 25 cm wide and 20 cm deep (10 x 8 in) with a flap of 12 cm and a handle 4 cm wide and 70 cm long (1½ x 28 in).

1

Knit two pieces:
1 x 52 x 25 cm
(21 x 10 in)
1 x 4 cm (1½ in)
x 70 cm (28 in).

2

Press lightly.
Turn up 20 cm (8 in) of the larger piece and sew up the sides.

3

Turn right side out. Pin the long handle piece across the side seam allowing an 8 cm (3 in) overlap. Sew on the handle using the same coloured yarn and small straight stitches on the outside. Add extra stitches on the inside at the top for strength.

tip:

When joining in a new yarn tie the new yarn through the first stitch of the row and continue knitting using the new yarn.

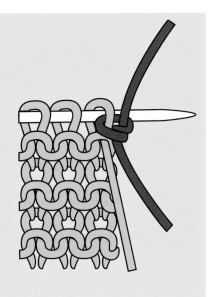

Project: 03
Bags continued

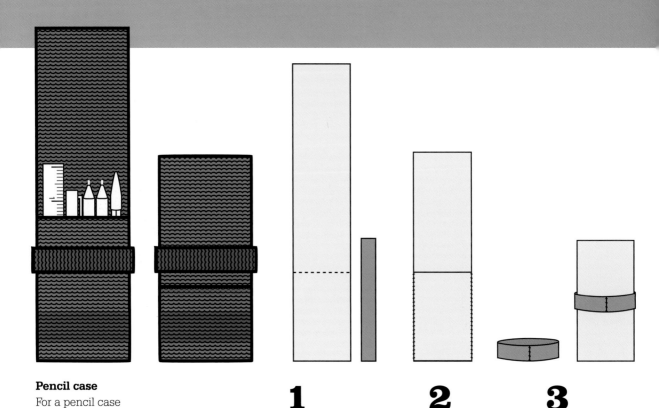

Pencil case
For a pencil case measuring 14 x 8 cm (5½ x 3 in).

1
Knit two pieces:
1 x 40 x 8cm
(15¾ x 3 in)
1 x 16.5 x 2cm
(6½ x ¾ in).

2
Press lightly.
Turn up 12 cm
(4¾ in) and sew up the sides.

3
Sew up the strap ends. Secure strap at the back with a couple of stitches.

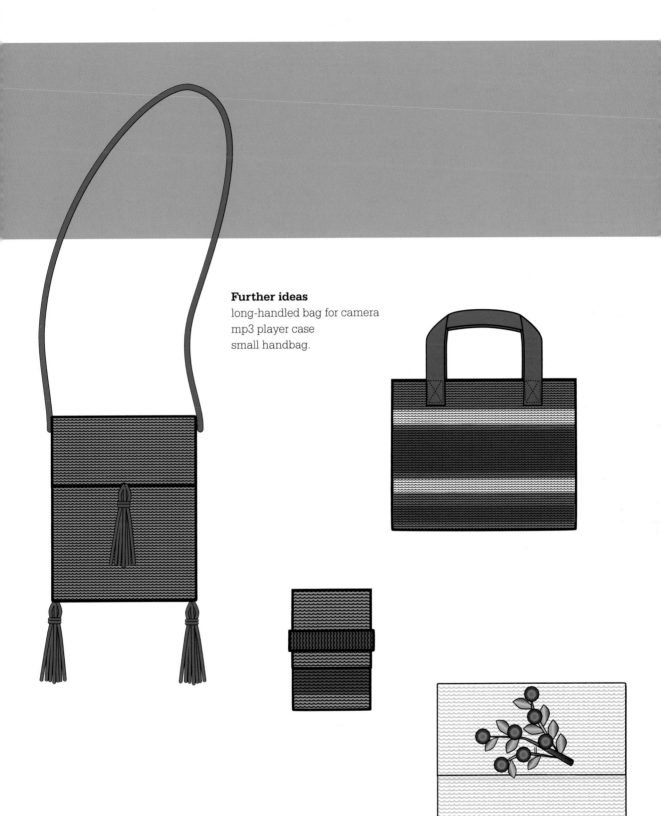

Further ideas
long-handled bag for camera
mp3 player case
small handbag.

Project: 04 Monkey

Everyone loves a soft toy and this one is suitable for all ages. Although it is made up of quite a few pieces they are all rectangles so this monkey is very easy and quick to make.

Knit 10 pieces

2 x ears 6 x 4 cm (2½ x 1½ in)
1 x nose 4 x 6 cm (1½ x 2½ in)
1 x body/head 8 x 44 cm (3¼ x 17 in)
2 x legs 8 x 30 cm (3¼ x 12 in)
2 x arms 6 x 24 cm (2½ x 9½ in)
1 x tail 4 x 35 cm (1½ x 13¾ in)
1 x scarf 3 x 45 cm (1½ x 18 in)

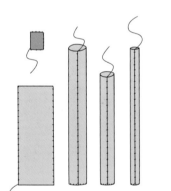

Sew

Sew up the sides of the body/head. Sew up the back seam and bottom edge of the legs, arms and tail. Sew round three sides of the ears leaving one long side open.

Stuff

Turn right side out and stuff. Use a synthetic toy filling so that the monkey can be washed.

Assemble

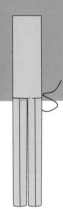

1

Attach the legs to the body using small stitches and sewing through from front to back.

2

Form the head by running a gathering thread through 8 cm (3¼ in) from the top. Pull gently to form a neck, wind the yarn round a few times, tie securely and thread the ends into the body so that they can't come undone.

3

Attach the arms to the side of the body to form shoulders. Stitch underneath so that the stitches don't show. Attach the ears from the back and stitch on the tail.

4

Sew three sides of the nose to the face. Fill with enough stuffing to form a gentle bump. Sew up the remaining side.

tip:

Stuffing long thin tubes can be tricky so it's best to feed the stuffing in gradually in small amounts. Use a chunky, round-ended knitting needle to poke the stuffing into the corners – but do it gently.

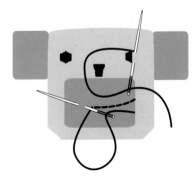

Finish off
Add eyes and a nose using straight satin stitch (see page 37).

Project: 05
Blankets, throws & cushions

Anyone can make a blanket or a cushion cover from knitted squares, but if you are clever and make a plan you can create some pretty stylish stuff.

Just by working simple two-colour stripes, and then varying the direction of these stripes when joining together the squares, you can achieve a variety of effects.

tip:

Keep the squares flat when you are sewing them together and don't make the stitches too tight.

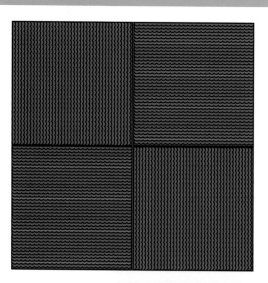

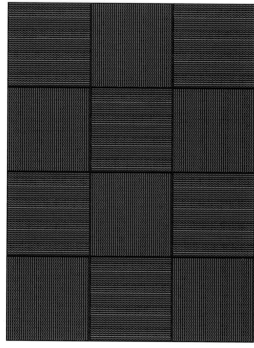

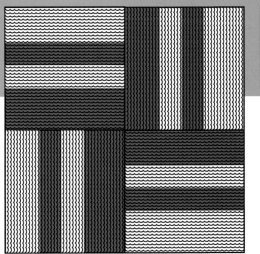

Project: 06
Trimmings

Easy-to-make pom-poms and tassels can cheer up a plain hat, bag or cushion and creative types can turn skinny, twisted lengths of knitting into unusual jewellery or trimmings.

Pom-pom

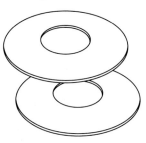

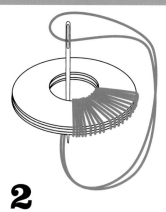

1

Cut out two cardboard discs each with a hole in the centre.

2

Thread long lengths of yarn onto a large needle and wind the wool round the two discs until the card is well covered.

3

Insert the blade of a pair of scissors between the two cardboard discs and snip through the strands of yarn.

4

Pull the discs a little way apart and wind a long length of yarn several times round the middle pulling it tight as you go. Knot securely and leave a length for tying.

5

Remove the cardboard discs and shake the pom-pom into shape.

Tassel 1

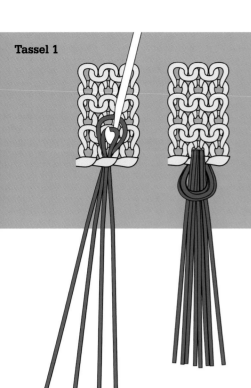

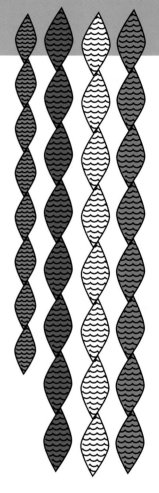

1

Cut several lengths of yarn and with the wrong side of the work facing and using a crochet hook, pull each one through a stitch to form a loop.

2

Turn to the right side, take the yarn ends and pull them through the loop.

3

Tug the strands down and pull up the loop to form a knot. Trim the ends.

Tassel 2

Cut several lengths of yarn and tie them together in the middle. Hold the strands firmly and bind them together by winding a length of yarn tightly and neatly around the bunch. Tie securely and poke the ends through to form extra strands. Trim the tassel ends. Use the original tie to sew or tie into place.

Twisted strands

Cast on a very small number of stitches (4-6) and keep knitting every row. The thin lengths will form natural spirals. Knit several and use them to make necklaces and bracelets.

Sewing

Don't be put off by talk of tacking, turnings and seam allowances, they are not all that complicated and once you have mastered the basics you can make all sorts of stuff including great bags and cushions.

Sewing

If you are already familiar with basic sewing techniques you can skip these pages, but for those who may never have threaded a needle knowing how to do a few basic stitches will enable you to tackle some of the simple projects.

Stitches

These basic stitches are all you need in order to make the projects in this book. In certain circumstances, especially seams and some edges, machine sewing is best but if you don't have a sewing machine it is still possible to make everything by hand.

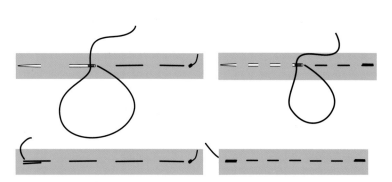

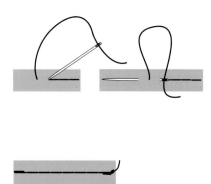

Tacking stitch

A long, loose stitch used for temporarily keeping fabric in place before machining or hemming. The stitches are big so that they can be pulled out easily.

Start and finish: Tacking is temporary so just tie a knot in the thread at the beginning and at the end work a couple of back stitches. Keep the knot and the ends to the right side so that you can pull them out easily.

Running stitch

A smaller, neater form of tacking. It is not suitable for seams but is used for quilting and gathering.

Start and finish: Sew 3 or 4 small back stitches at the beginning and the end. For extra security tie a knot in the thread when starting.

Back stitch

Use this stitch for seams if you don't have a sewing machine. Keep the stitches neat and straight to keep your seams neat and straight.

Start and finish: Sew 3 or 4 small back stitches at the beginning and the end (but don't make them too tight or the fabric will ruckle).

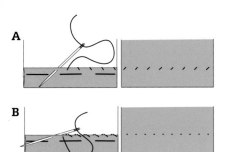

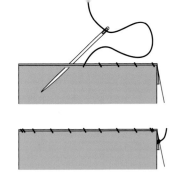

Hem stitch

Used for sewing up hems and edges. You can use a sewing machine instead but in some circumstances a hand-sewn hem stitch is better as it is less visible. Hand hemming is also better for soft or lightweight fabrics. A produces diagonal stitches on the right side, if you want a less visible stitch use B.

Start and finish: Sew several small stitches on the inside edge only at the beginning and the end. Leave ends of at least 2 cm (¾ in) and tuck them out of sight.

Oversewing

This is a form of hem stitch used to sew two edges together. It is used for sewing up the gap after turning a piece of work right side out. In this instance the stitches will be visible on both sides so make them as small as possible. This stitch is also used in patchwork for hand sewing the pieces together.

Start and finish: Tie a knot in the end of the thread and sew a few small back stitches. Finish with more small stitches and tuck the end through to the back.

Machine stitching

Machining produces a strong, even line of stitching which is preferable for seams. It is used to add extra strength along edges and can also be used to add decorative detail on pockets and hems. Modern sewing machines have extra functions including zig-zag stitching which can also be used as decoration.

Start and finish: Use the reverse action to sew a few short stitches at the beginning and the end of a row. Snip off the ends leaving a small amount of thread. Pull the ends on the right side through to the wrong side. Alternatively you can leave long ends and tie them by hand. Pull the thread on the right side to the wrong side, tie the ends together and trim but not too close to the knot.

tip:

An iron is a very useful tool for stitchers. You will get a neater and more accurate finish if you press seams and edges at all stages of sewing. You can use it to turn in edges but as most fabrics are naturally stretchy this can lead to inaccuracies so sometimes it is best to pin first.

Hem stitch, Oversewing, Machine stitching

Hems

The raw edges of fabric are normally turned in. This not only looks neater but also stops the fabric from fraying. For a hem the fabric is turned in twice. The first fold hides the raw edge and is normally quite narrow. The second turning is wider and the edges are sewn down either by hand using hem stitch or stitched down using a sewing machine. For most of the projects in this book the suggested amount for first turning is 7.5 cm (¼ in).

Seam allowance

A seam is what you get when you sew two pieces of fabric together. The width between the fabric edge and the seam stitching is known as an 'allowance' and this must be wide enough to prevent the seam pulling apart and to allow for the fact that raw edges fray which can also weaken a seam. When working out measurements these allowances need to be added on.

For most of the projects in this book the suggested seam allowance is 1.5 cm (⅝ in). This is quite generous but is suitable for the types of fabric suggested and makes accuracy a little less crucial if you are not a practised machinist. For smaller items or finer fabrics the allowance can be smaller.

Seams should be straight so if you are not confident that you can keep a straight line draw it on the fabric with tailor's chalk or a chalk pencil.

Sewing a seam

 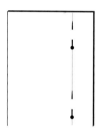 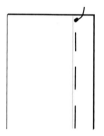 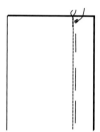

1
Measure the seam allowance from the fabric's raw edge. Mark the measured seam line with a chalk pencil.

2
Pin the two pieces of fabric together along the marked seam line.

3
Tack the two pieces keeping the stitches to one side of the seam line to allow room for the final stitching.

4
Machine or hand sew along the seam line.

tip:

If you are stitching two pieces of fabric together around two or more sides trim the corners (not too near to the stitching). This makes it easier to get neat corners when you turn it right side out.

Making a hem

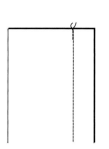  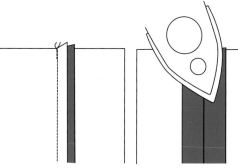 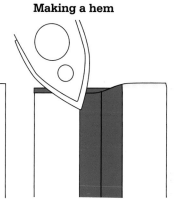

5
Remove the tacking stitches.

6
Open up the seam.

7
Press the seam flat.

8
Press down the first turning.

  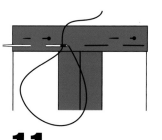 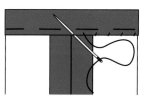

9
Make the second turning and press down.

10
Pin into place (for short lengths you can miss this out and go straight to tacking).

11
Tack the turnings in postiton.

12
Hand or machine stitch the hem edge.

Project: 07
Easy stuff

You can make lots of useful and good-looking things from squares and rectangles of fabric that only require turning in and hemming. If you want to keep it small go for napkins or even handkerchiefs and you could always turn that odd piece of special fabric into a scarf. Go bigger and whip up a chef's apron, and if you are into interiors make a simple curtain.

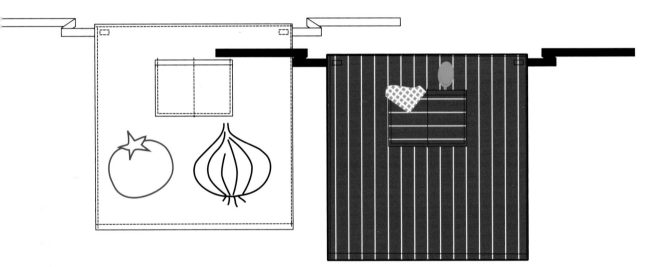

Make a chef's apron

The classic chef's apron measures 92 x 92 cm (36 x 36 in) but this measurement is not crucial and may need adjusting for different sized bodies.

Use a thick cotton fabric and allow for turnings at the top and sides of 1 cm (⅜ in) for the first turning with the second turning of 1.5 cm (⅝ in) and 1 cm (⅜ in) and 5 cm (2 in) along the bottom. Machine or hand sew.

A good size for a pocket is 36 x 25 cm (14 x 10 in) plus turnings. When sewing on to the apron front add a line of stitching in the middle to divide it into two pockets.

Ties made from the same fabric can end up too stiff and bulky so use a strong cotton tape (which you can find in haberdashery departments) instead.

Personalise and decorate to taste using ideas from other pages in the book.

Make some table napkins

The average size for napkins is 45 x 45cm (18 x 18 in).
Allowing for a first turning 0.5 cm (¼ in) and 1 cm (⅜ in)
for the second, you will need a square measuring 48 x 48
cm (19½ x 19½ in) but you can vary this size to suit. The
hems can be finished by hand or machine. If you have a
machine with embroidery stitches you could use these to
make decorative edges. Add extra decoration in the form
of appliqué (see page 58) or create your own patterns
and prints (see pages 154-159).

Make a café curtain

Make simple café curtain by sewing round a rectangle
of fabric and fixing it to a wire strung across a window
using clothes-pegs.

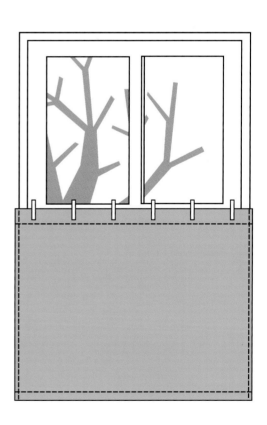

tip:

**If you are hemming
lightweight fabrics make the
turnings smaller and tack in
place before sewing by hand.**

Project: 08
Sewing kit

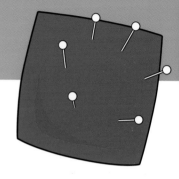

Make a pincushion

For a small pincushion measuring 10 x 10 cm (4 x 4 in).
Cut two pieces 11 x 11 cm (4¼ x 4¼ in).

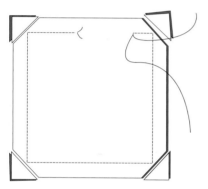

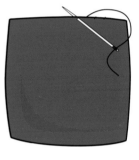

1

With right side facing sew the pieces together leaving a gap so that you can turn it right side out.
Trim the corners.

2

Turn the side out. Stuff with enough filler to make the pincushion as fat as possible.

3

Over-stitch the gap to close.

Make it a bracelet pincushion

Make it a bracelet pincushion by sewing on a strap of wide elastic. Take the measurements from your own wrist (don't make it too tight) then stitch the strap to the back of the pincushion. Check that the pincushion is fat enough to stop the pins sticking into you.

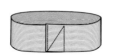

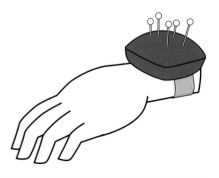

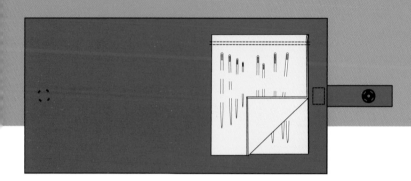

Make a needle case

Cut two pieces 20 x 11 cm
(8¼ x 4¼ in).
Sew together as for the pincushion
but omit stuffing it with filling.
Cut two pieces of felt 8 x 6 cm
(3 x 2¼ in) and stitch them into the
case as shown.
Sew on a strap fastened with
a press stud or snap fastener.

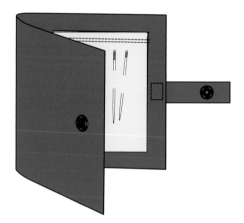

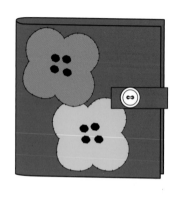

Get creative

Customise your pincushion or
needlecase with decorative appliqué
or embroidery.

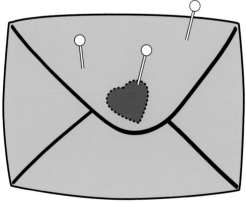

Handles, straps & pockets

Make a handle

Straps and handles need to be strong. For shorter length you can sew two pieces of fabric together and turn them right side out but with long, narrow lengths this can be very tricky so this folded method is easier.

Suggested dimensions:

For a strap 2.5 cm (1 in) wide you will need a long piece of fabric 5.5 cm (4¼ in) wide. The length is up to you but standard lengths are 70 cm (27½ in) for a shoulder strap and 40 cm (16 in) for a short handle. Add 11 cm (4½ in) for turnings at top and bottom and for attaching.

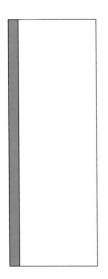

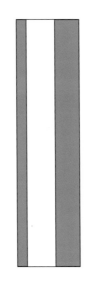

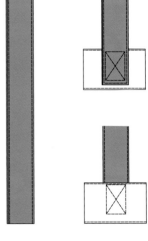

1

Cut a piece of fabric 5.5 cm (2¼ in) wide and length to suit.
Fold in 1 cm (⅜ in) along one side. Press.

2

Fold in 2 cm (¾ in) along other side. Press.

3

Turn over 1cm (⅜ inch) at the top and bottom. Press. Fold in half. Press. Pin the edges together and tack in place (you can miss out the tacking if you are a good machinist).

4

Machine along the folded edge and continue round the other three edges. Sew to the inside of the bag as above, using reinforcing stitches.

Fasten that bag

Make a basic tote bag more secure with a closure. Follow the instructions as for the strap but make it wider. Sew it on at the back as you would a handle. Fasten with press studs or snap fasteners or hook and loop tape (cover the stitches with a button or decoration), or be inventive with a pin. Personalise with a design or monogram.

Make a pocket

1

Cut a piece of fabric the size of the pocket required adding a turning allowance of 1 cm (⅜ in) at sides and bottom and 3 cm (1¼ in) at the top.

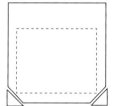

2

Trim the bottom corners as shown. This will make the turning in step 3 neater and less bulky.

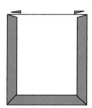

3

Turn in 1 cm (⅜ in) on sides and bottom edges. Trim small triangles off the top edge turning.

4

Fold over 1 cm (⅜ in) at the top.

5

Fold over 2 cm (¾ in) at the top and pin or tack in place. Hem the edge by hand or machine. Machine stitching can become a decorative feature as shown here.

6

Pin and tack the pocket in place.

7

Stitch round the sides and bottom edge of the pocket.

tip:

To strengthen the pocket and prevent it from coming undone extend the final stitching to just beyond the pocket edges and add extra stitches at the corners.

Project: 09
Make a basic tote bag

You can never have too many bags and simple tote bags are easy to sew. Make them in bright fabrics and bold prints or make plain ones as a blank canvas on which to show off your wit, beliefs and design skills. Draw up your own designs using fabric pens, decorate with potato prints or show off your embroidery skills with appliqué, cross stitch and quilting.

Customise your creations with pockets, make the handles and straps just the right size for you and secure them with simple fastenings and secret compartments.

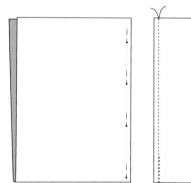

1
Cut a piece of fabric 44 x 134 cm (17½ x 53 in). Fold and pin together the sides.

2
Sew up the sides with a seam allowance of 2 cm (¾ in).

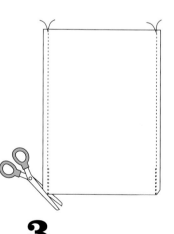

3
Trim the bottom corners.

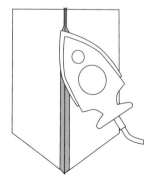

4
Press open the seams.

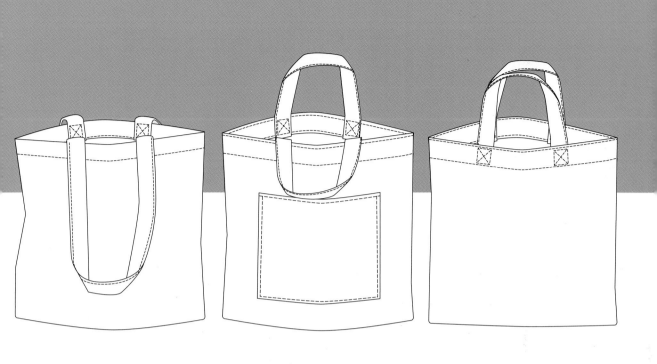

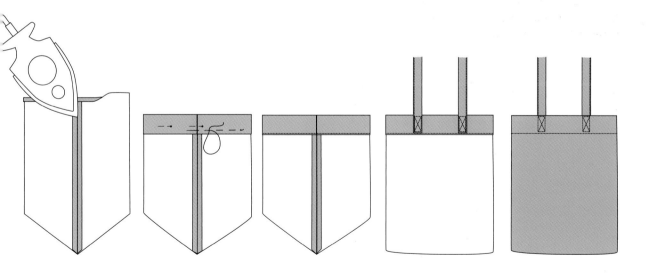

5

Turn over 1 cm (⅜ in) around the top edge and press.

6

Turn over another 6 cm (2½ in) around the top edge. Pin down then tack in position.

7

Stitch around the turning along the bottom edge.

8

Sew on the handles with reinforced stitching.

9

Turn right side out and press.

Project: 10 Make a duffel bag

An alternative to the knapsack the duffel bag is very easy to make. Personalise it with bespoke pockets and decorate with your own hand-stitched badges and charms.

1

To make a bag measuring approx 35 x 40 cm (13¾ x 15¾ in)
Cut one piece of fabric 73 x 47 cm (28¾ x 18½ in).
Cut one piece of fabric 6 x 12 cm (2⅓ x 4¾ in).
Eyelet kit.
2.5 m (2¾ yds) of cord.

2

Turn over 1 cm (⅜ in) along the top.

3

Turn over a further 4 cm (1⅔ in) and stitch along the top and bottom edges of the turning.

4

Following the instructions on the pack insert eyelets at regular invervals. Remember to leave enough space at the sides for sewing up the seam.

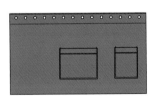

5

Make pockets to the required size (see page 43). Pin, tack and sew in position.

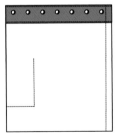

6

Fold in half with right sides facing and sew up the side seam.

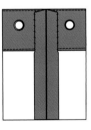

7

For a neat appearance fold in the edges of the seam at the top and stitch down.

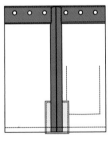

8

Fold so that the seam is at the centre of the back. Insert the eyelet tag upside down between the two right sides and sew along the bottom.

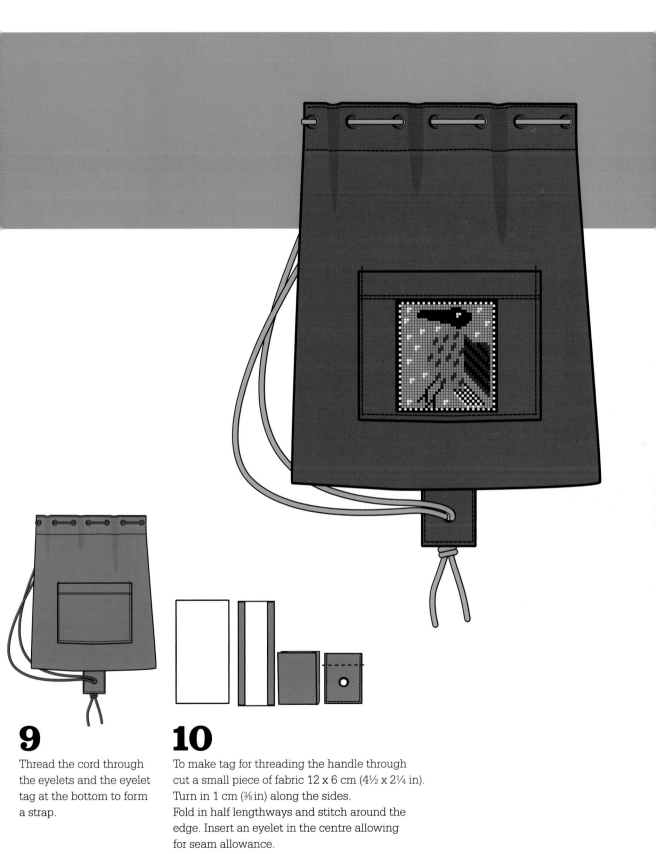

9

Thread the cord through the eyelets and the eyelet tag at the bottom to form a strap.

10

To make tag for threading the handle through cut a small piece of fabric 12 x 6 cm (4½ x 2¼ in). Turn in 1 cm (⅜ in) along the sides. Fold in half lengthways and stitch around the edge. Insert an eyelet in the centre allowing for seam allowance.

Project: 11
Make a cushion cover

This cushion cover is made from one piece of fabric and requires no zips or ties.

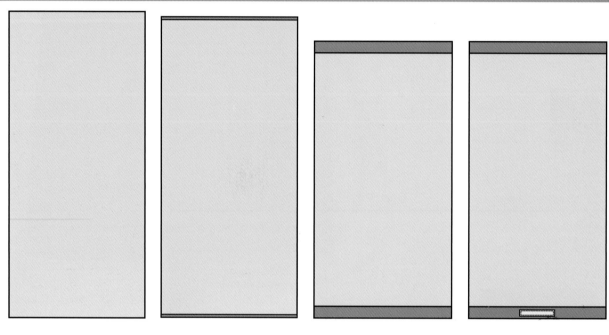

1

Cut a piece of fabric 102 x 48 cm (40¼ x 19 in).

2

Turn in 1 cm (⅜ in) at top and bottom.

3

Turn in 5 cm (2 in) at top and bottom, stitch along the top and bottom of the turning.

4

With wrong side facing sew one part of a 7cm (3 in) length of hook and loop tape and stick in the centre of the bottom hem.

5

With right side facing sew the other part of the hook and loop tape on the top hem.

6

Stick the two pieces of hook and loop tape together and fold in half.

7

Stitch down the two sides and trim corners.

8

Turn right side out. Stuff in the cushion pad and fasten with the hook and loop tape.

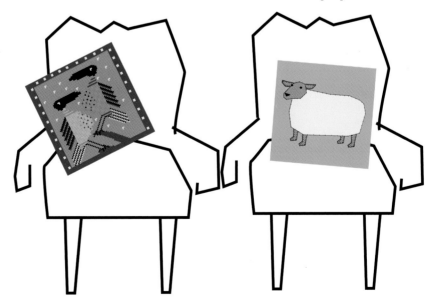

Project: 12 Make a laundry bag

Drawstring bags can be any size and can have any number of uses. Make a large one for your laundry or smaller ones for socks or shoes. Make a tiny one, fill it with lavender and hang it in your wardrobe to ward off moths.

To make a bag measuring 50 x 60 cm (19⅔ x 23⅔ in).
Cut one piece fabric 134 x 53 cm (52¾ x 20 in).
2.5 m cord (2¾ yds).

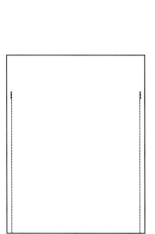 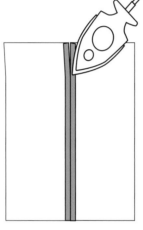 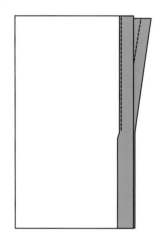 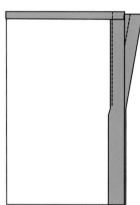

1

Fold in half lengthways and sew up the side seams leaving a gap of 12 cm (4¾ in) unstitched at the top.

2

Fold back and press the unstitched edge.

3

Turn in the unstitched edges and hem either by hand or machine.

4

Turn over 1 cm (⅜ in) around the top edge.

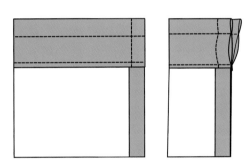

5

Turn over 4 cm (1½ in) and stitch one row of stitches 2 cm (¾ in) from the top and another row along the folded edge to create a channel through which to thread the cord.

6

Thread the cord through the channel twice, tie the loose ends together then cut and tie the looped end.

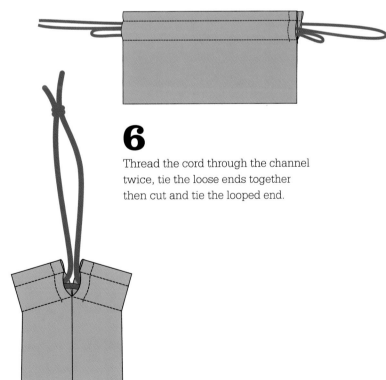

Project: 13
Make a
fabric kit roll

Keep your kit in order and store it in a fabric roll.
The size depends on what you want to store.
To work out the measurements lay out your kit
and draw a pattern. Allow enough room so that
things don't poke out at the top and don't make
the individual pockets too tight a fit.

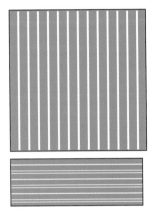

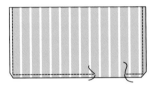
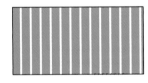

1

To make a roll measuring
approx 20 x 10 cm
(7¾ x 4 in).
Cut one piece of fabric
43 x 43 cm (17 x 17 in).
Cut one piece of fabric
10 x 43 cm (4 x 17 in).

2

Fold the larger piece in half
lengthways. Sew round
the edges but leave a gap
in the stitching so that you
can turn it right side out.
Trim the corners.

3

Turn right side out. Press.
Turn in the unstitched
edges and overstitch the
gap closed.

4

Make the inside pocket
as on page 43. Mark the
position of further dividing
lines using a chalk pencil.

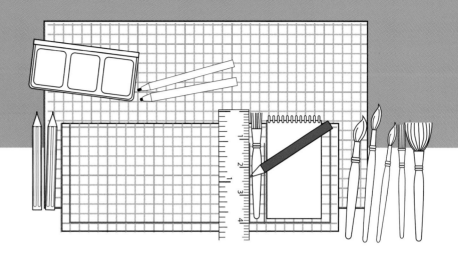

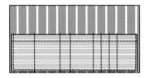

5

Tack in place, stitch the pocket onto the back piece and then stitch along the dividing lines to form the mini pockets.

6

Attach a length of tape, cord or ribbon long enough to wrap round the roll and tie in a bow.

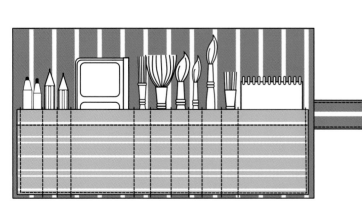

An alternative fastening is a strap secured with a press stud or snap fastener or hook and loop tape. The length of the strap will depend on the size of your roll and how fat it will be when rolled up but as a rough guide cut a piece the same length as the roll. Turn in the sides and top, fold in half and stitch round the edges.

Stitching

Stitching isn't all fancy needlework and complicated patterns. Learn the basics and apply your own style to turn traditional needlework into something you are happy to show off.

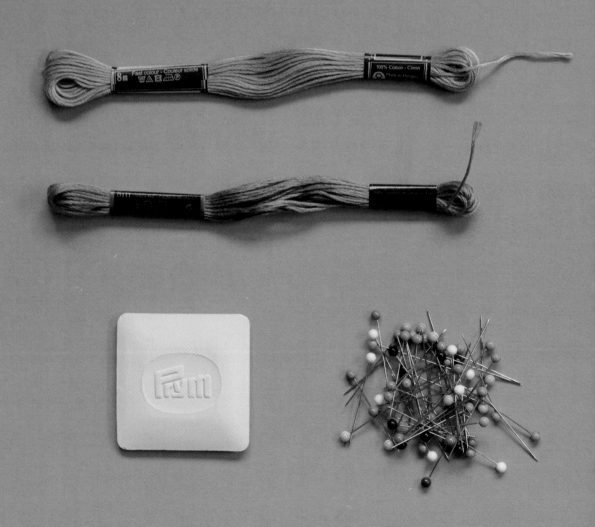

Stitching

Stitching isn't all fancy stitches, complicated techniques and twee patterns. Learn the basics and apply your own style to turn traditional needlework into something you are happy to show off.

This chapter covers appliqué, quilting, patchwork, cross stitch and tapestry. The world of embroidery contains many hundreds of stitches and techniques and quite a few rules, but here you will find that knowing only the simplest and most basic is no barrier to creating lively stuff and so should encourage rather than deter would-be stitchers. You don't have to stick to one form of needlework, but can use several in one piece of work. For example, you can add quilting to your appliqué and then incoporate the design in a larger work such as a patchwork cushion or quilt. Sew your cross-stitch and tapestry creations on to bags and cushions or on to a pocket or T-shirt.

Choose colours carefully. Don't go mad, stick to a relatively small palette of two or three colours which are similar in tone with one brighter colour for contrast and highlight. For subtle and unexpected results try just using black and white with perhaps the odd flash of bright red or yellow.

Two useful stitches

These two stitches are a useful addition to the basics shown in the Sewing chapter.

Blanket stitch

Blanket stitch is a decorative edging which can be used instead of hem stitch or machining. It can be used on raw edges to give an interesting decorative effect and is useful if you don't want the bother of turning in the edges. Use ordinary, thin cotton thread if you don't want it to show up or thicker, colourful wool or thread if you do.

This stitch can also be used for sewing together two pieces of fabric and is also often used as a decorative detail on clothes – use it to cheer up an old coat.

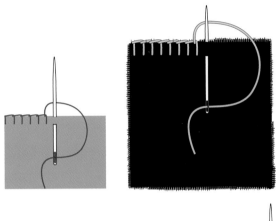

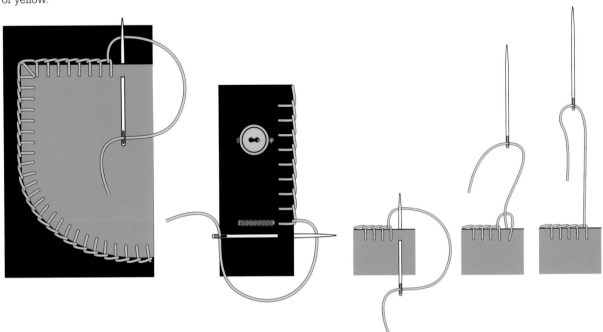

Satin stitch

Satin stitch is a straight stitch useful for stitching in small details such as eyes, noses, stalks and leaves but which can also be used as a decorative stitch as part of a design. Use it for lettering as shown here to add a classy monogram or to sign your own work. Don't worry too much about getting the stitches absolutely neat and accurate – a bit of unevenness adds character. You can do fine work with fine threads but you can also use embroidery threads and chunky wools.

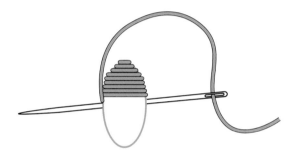

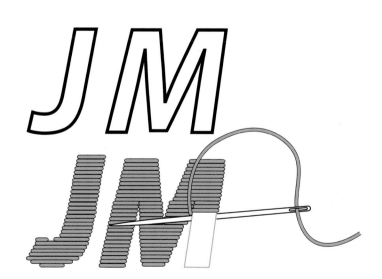

How to do appliqué

Appliqué involves sewing pieces of fabric onto a base fabric. It can be used as a form of decoration on anything from cushions and pillowcases to quilts and wall-hangings. The technique is very simple, you just cut out a shape and sew it down. Mostly the edges are turned in to give a neat finish which won't fray, but you can also leave the edges raw for a different sort of look.

The sewing down can be done by hand using hem stitch or blanket stitch or by machine. Hand sewing is best for complicated shapes but if you are handy with a machine you can make the machine stitching part of the design, using zig-zags for example. However, if you do prefer machining make sure the stitches are not too tight as this can cause puckering which will spoil the effect.

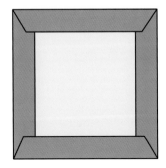

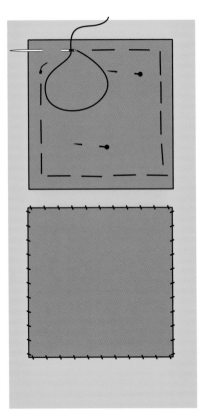

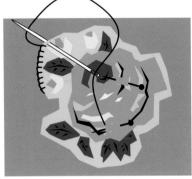

tip:

Skip the design stage and cut instant motifs from patterned fabrics.

The technique is simple – cut out a shape, turn it in, tack it down, sew it on.

Getting started Appliqué

1

Make a paper pattern by drawing (or printing) the required shape onto a piece of paper. Add an allowance all round for turning in. Cut out.

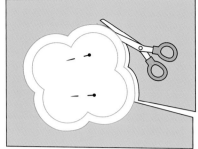

2

Pin the pattern on to the appliqué fabric and cut out the required shape.

3

Snip out small wedges from the turning allowance to make turning in easier.

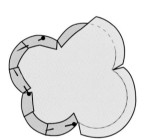

4

Turn in the edges (for complicated shapes you may want to pin or tack down the turnings as you go).

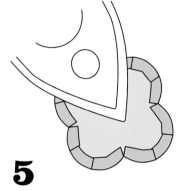

5

Press.

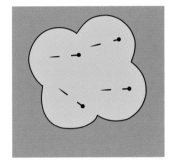

6

Pin the appliqué shape into position on the base fabric.

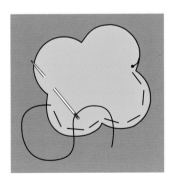

7

Tack down.

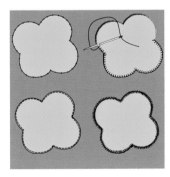

8

Sew down using hem stich, blanket stitch or machine stitches.

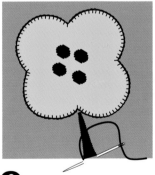

9

Add details using satin stitch or other embroidery stitches.

Project: 14 Make an appliqué sheep

For more complex motifs made up of several pieces it's important to sew them down in the right order.

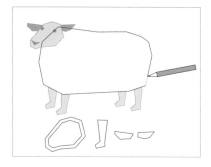

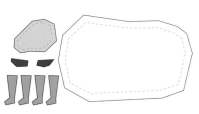

1

Make a paper pattern by drawing round each part. Add a turning in allowance to the head and body approximately 1 cm (⅜ in) all round. As the legs and ears are quite small making turnings on the edges is very fiddly so cut them to actual size.

2

Pin the pattern on to fabric and cut out.

3

Make small nicks in the edges of the turning allowance to make turning in easier.

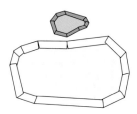

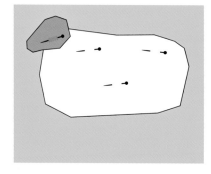

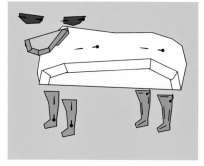

4

Turn in the edges and press (pin and tack if necessary).

5

Pin the body in place on the backing fabric and pin the head on top.

6

Plot the position of the ears and legs and pin and tack down.

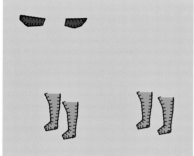

7

Remove the head and body pieces and blanket stitch around the legs and ears.

8

Pin and tack down the body piece with the head piece positioned on top.

9

Stitch down the body and head pieces.

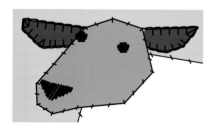

10

Add the eyes and nose detail using satin stitch (see page 57).

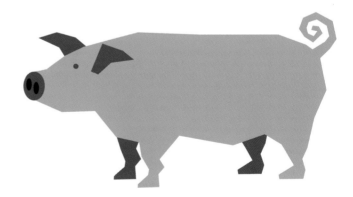

Now try a pig.

Project: 15 Make some fabric art

Making fabric pictures isn't new but your interpretation will be. Make your own designs and patterns from your own artwork. Inspiration can come from a variety of sources from paintings, the design world, old teapots or vintage fabrics.

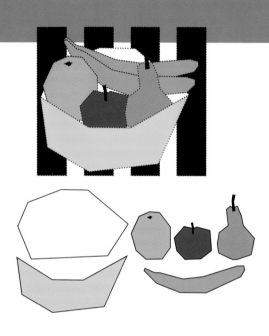

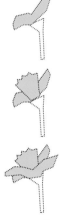

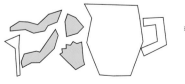

Don't be afraid to draw round stuff on postcards or in photographs and use scanning and computer programmes to manipulate images – and you don't have to restrict yourself to fabrics, appliqué can be part of an artwork that involves transfers and printing (see pages 148 and 156).

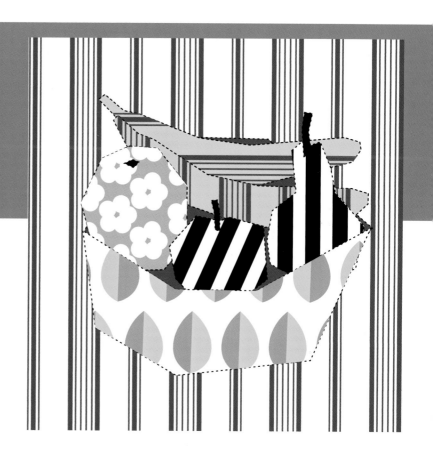

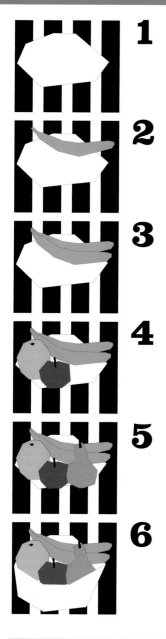

1

2

3

4

5

6

Why not transfer a photo on to some fabric, add a cheeky appliqué hat and sew it on to a bag or a cushion, or just as a picture.

How to quilt

Quilting gives a raised effect and involves stitching a sandwich made up from two pieces of fabric with a padded filling. There are various styles of quilting some of which are very complex and require a high level of skill, but the projects here are simple to do, and though most recommend using a sewing machine you can still achieve interesting results with hand stitching.

The filling in the sandwich is called padding, wadding or batting and can vary from relatively thin, which gives a subtle quilt effect, to deeper wadding which gives a more puffy look. Wadding is normally sold in sheet form from a roll like fabric and there is a choice of cotton, wool and polyester. Polyester is cheap and easy to use but the bits of fibre do tend to poke through with use. Wool produces a great look but is not easily washable. Cotton is a good compromise, it is a natural fibre and easy to work with.

If you are quilting small items or working with appliqué you can use a loose, synthetic filling instead.

Machine stitching can be used for added strength as well as decoration. Straight lines can be used for a variety of patterns and effects. For accuracy draw in guide lines with a chalk pencil.

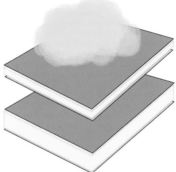

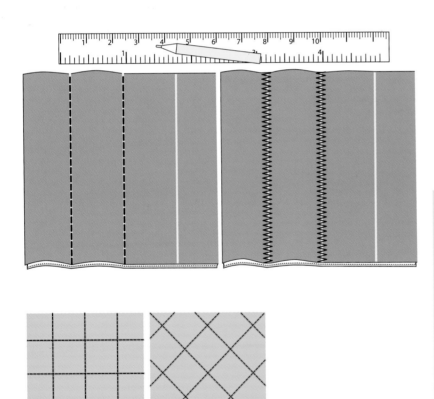

tip:

If you are making a large quilt an easier alternative to wadding is to use an inexpensive fleece rug or even an old blanket.

Quick quilt

Use a fleece blanket as a template. Cut the front and back fabrics 1 cm (⅜ in) larger all round so that when the 'sandwich' is stitched together the fleece is stitched in but doesn't extend to the edges. This makes the seams less bulky.

With the right sides of the front and back fabrics facing place the fleece on top and stitch all round quite near to the edge of the fleece leaving a gap along the bottom edge for turning right side out.

Turn right side out, press gently and oversew the gap to close. Sew several rows of tacking stitches across and down to keep everything in place when it is being stitched.

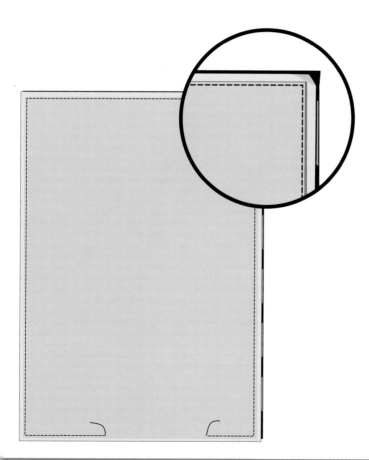

The next stage is to add rows of quilting stitches which can be done by hand or using a machine. A line of stitching all round the edge gives a finished look – do it first and then use it as a guide for where to begin and end the rows of quilting stitches.

tip:

If you are using a patterned fabric use the pattern as a guide for the lines of quilting.

Hand stitching

Hand stitching obviously takes longer but it is a pleasant pastime and produces a softer finish than machine stitching and is ideal for small projects. If you don't want to tackle anything too large or too taxing put a simple image on a small square of fabric, make a sandwich with a piece of wadding and a backing fabric, stitch around the design and use it for patchwork or a whimsical badge.

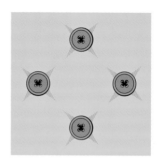

You can quilt with buttons and knots.
The buttons can be any shape or size.
Use thick coloured thread for the knots and make sure they are tied securely.

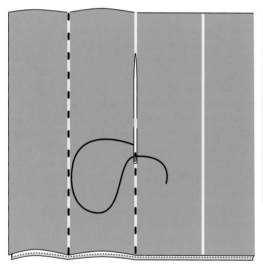

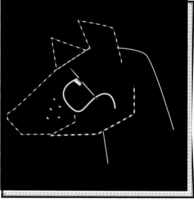

1

Make a pattern and cut out the shape with a turning allowance all round.

2

Cut a piece of wadding the size of the finished shape and position it on the wrong side of the fabric.

3

Fold the edges over the wadding (tack in place if necessary).

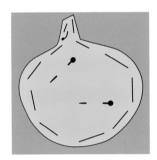

4

Pin and tack onto background.

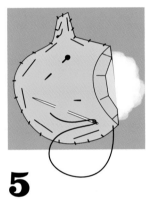

5

or ... for a fatter result leave out the wadding and stuff with filling.

6

Stitch in place.

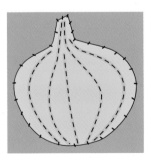

7

Quilt with lines of stitching.

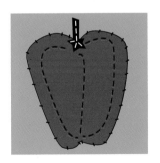

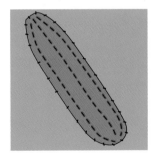

Quilt some vegetables

Project: 16
Make a laptop case

Protect your laptop by slipping it into a quilted zip-up case bag before popping it in your bag. This design includes a zipper but the method used makes it easy to put in.

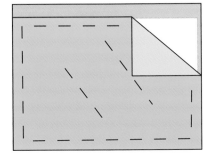

1

Laptop sizes vary and some are thinner than others so make a paper pattern by drawing round the laptop. Measure the height of the laptop and add this measurement to the width and then add a further 3 cm (1¼ in) seam allowance.
For the length add the height of the laptop plus 7 cm (2¾ in) for the bottom seam and top turnings.

Cut main piece using the measurements above.

Cut out a lining which is 3 cm (1¼ in) shorter at the top.

Cut the wadding so that it is 1 cm (⅜ in) smaller at sides and bottom and 4 cm (1⅔ in) shorter at top.

2

Place the wadding on the wrong side of the large piece of fabric (the front) so that there is a margin of 1 cm (⅜ in) around side and bottom edges.

3

Place the lining right side up on top of the wadding so that the sides and edges line up with the larger piece of fabric. Tack the sandwich together with a few extra lines of tacking stitches to keep the fabric and wadding in place when it is quilted.

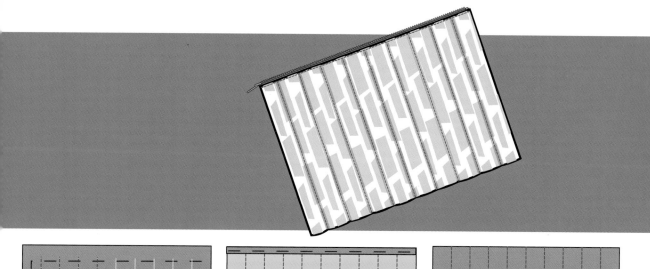

4

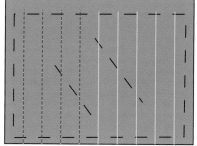

With the right side of the fabric facing, draw on guide lines using a chalk pencil or, if the fabric is patterned, use the pattern to plot the lines. Stitch along the guide lines stopping short of the top edge where the lining stops. Remove the tacking stitches.

5

With the lining facing turn over the top of the front fabric so that it covers the top edge of the lining. Tack down. Repeat for second piece of fabric and lining.

6

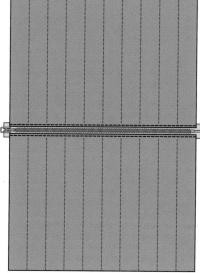

Place the zip right side up and lay the two pieces on top to either side as shown. Tack in position and stitch in place.

7

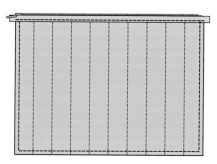

With wrong sides facing sew along the sides and bottom making sure that the wadding is stitched in.

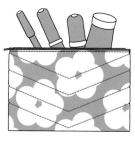

Now make smaller ones and use them for make-up, pencils, or love letters...

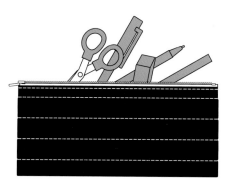

Project: 17 Make a patchwork cushion

Traditional patchwork can be a complicated, if enjoyable, business and keen patchworkers spend hours creating quite complex designs. However, it is possible to achieve good results using simple squares. Patches can be sewn together by hand or machine, or you can opt for the easy way which is a mixture of appliqué and patchwork.

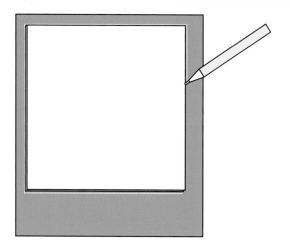

1
Make a square template from cardboard or stiff paper. The size depends on the finished size of the project and the design.

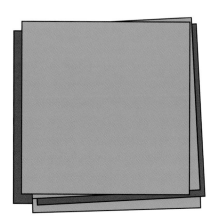

2
Draw around the template and cut out the fabric squares adding a 2 cm (¾ in) margin all the way around.

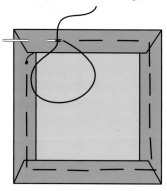

3
Turn in 2 cm (¾ in) all around and tack down.

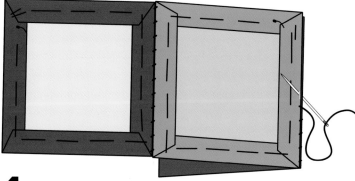

4
Oversew the squares together working from the back. It will be easier if you stitch them in rows and then join the rows together.

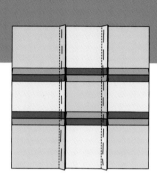

5

Tack together the patches in strips of three and sew the two seams as shown.

6

Remove the tacking and press open the seams on each row of three.

7

Tack then stitch together the three strips as shown.

8

Remove the tacking, open up the seams and press flat.

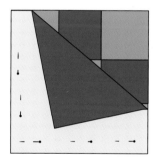

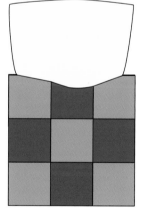

9

Cut a piece of fabric (or make both sides from patches if you wish) for the back of the cushion which is the same size as the front. With the right sides facing pin and tack the pieces together.

10

Sew around the edges leaving a gap for turning right side out that is big enough to get the cushion pad through.

11

Turn right side out, stuff in the cushion pad.

12

Sew up the gap.

Project: 18
Easy
patchwork

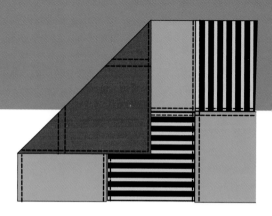

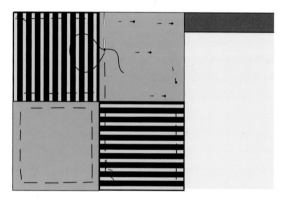

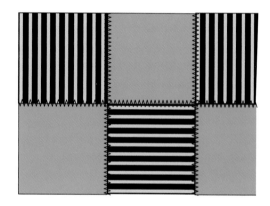

Instead of sewing each patch together cheat by laying the patches on to a backing fabric and sewing them down using a sewing machine, or if you prefer, by hand. The dimensions of each patch depends on the finished size of your chosen project and the number of patches required for the design. Thick cotton is a good fabric for backing – furnishing fabrics are ideal as they also come in generous widths. An alternative is to sew the patches onto a fleece or rug, or even a thin cotton dhurrie.

tip:

Don't forget to leave the knot and ends on top so that the tacking can be removed easily.

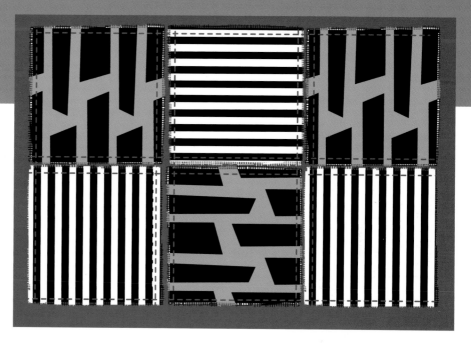

If you want an even easier option and a more characterful look don't bother with turnings and just sew the cut patches down on to the backing fabric in their raw-edged state. The stitching will prevent fraying. For an even more 'rustic' look sew the patches down by hand using a thick coloured thread.

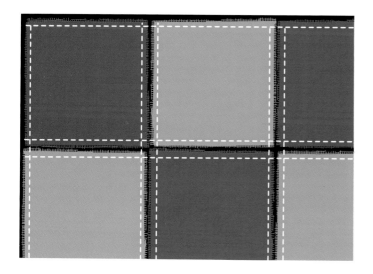

Project: 19
Go geometric

There are hundreds of designs for patchwork and some are very complicated. Although the designs here look complex, they are relatively simple to do using only three shapes. They may require a little more effort and careful planning, but the results can be quite spectacular. Depending on your skill and patience you can choose whether to sew by hand or machine or, the easiest option, to work the patterns as a form of appliqué.

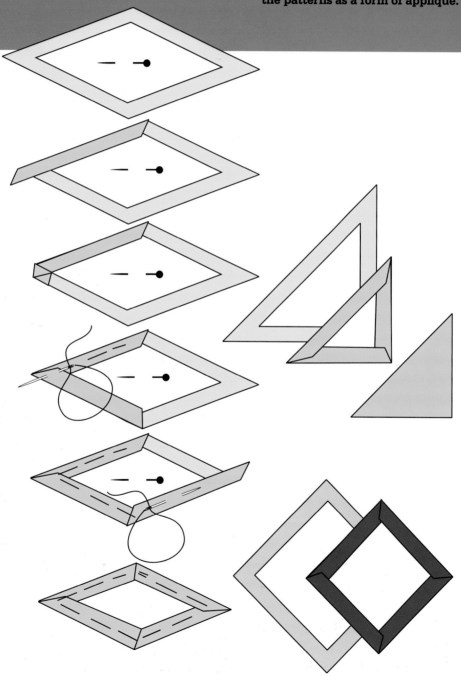

The sharp corners on diamond and triangle shapes are a bit more awkward to deal with and therefore require a little more preparation.

These three shapes form the building blocks to create an impressive range of optical effects.

Big stuff

Quilt-making is an old tradition which often involved groups of
people working on one quilt, so if you can't face doing it all yourself
you could turn it into a social activity involving friends and family.
If you haven't the patience for fiddly work you can always speed
things up by making your quilt from very large squares or even
long strips.

Cross stitch & tapestry

Cross stitch and tapestry (also called needlepoint) have been popular pastimes for centuries but a new take on the subject matter brings it right up to date.

Cross stitch fabric is normally a white or cream, floppy material with holes for forming the stitch. The stitches are done in stranded cotton also called 'floss' which is made up from 6 strands of thread. Most cross-stitch is done using three strands of thread so you have to divide the lengths of floss before using. Cross stitch is done using an embroidery needle which has a long eye for the embroidery thread.

Tapestry canvas is a stiffer fabric and is mostly a natural beige colour. Tapestry is worked with tapestry wool and a tapestry needle which has a large eye and a blunt, rounded end.

For both cross stitch and tapestry, the size of the stitch depends on the distance between the holes. The different sizes of cross stitch and tapestry materials are normally indicated as HPI – (holes per inch) also called count with 6 count being a large stitch and 22 count a very small stitch. Sizes in between include 10, 11, 12, 14 and 18. The basic cross stitch and tapestry stitches are easy to do. There are plenty of more complicated and fancy variations on these stitches but you can still produce unusual and distinctive designs using the simplest ones.

Patterns are created by following charts with each square denoting one stitch. In black and white charts the different colours are represented by symbols, but here the charts are in colour. You don't have to stick to the recommended colours and can create your own palette if you prefer. These charts can be used for both cross stitch and tapestry.

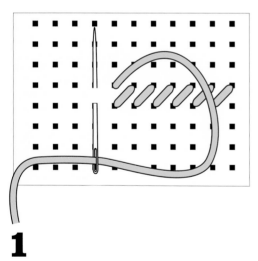

1
The most basic cross stitch is formed from two crossed diagonal stitches. Work all the right-slanting stitches first in a row.

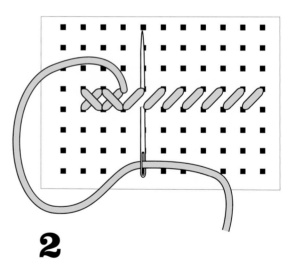

2
Then change direction and work all the left-slanting stitches to complete the 'cross'.

Although cross stitch and tapestry are treated as different disciplines, in haberdashery departments and websites, there can be quite a lot of crossover. For example you could choose to do chunky cross stitch using tapestry wool on tapestry canvas, and you could also use tapestry wool with a 6-count cross stitch fabric. You can also use stranded cotton on a fine tapestry canvas. Serious embroiderers may disapprove but if you want to use a mixture of cross-stitch and tapestry in one piece of work that's fine.

tip:

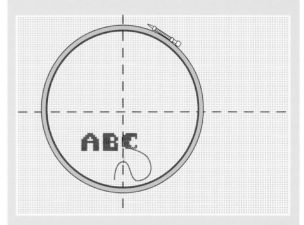

When starting a complicated design, stitch vertical and horizontal lines of tacking to mark the centre of the canvas or fabric and help you to follow the pattern.

For fine cross stitch using an embroidery frame will make it easier to sew even stitches.

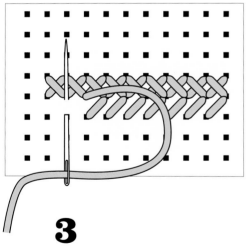

3

Try to keep the stitches even and don't pull the thread through too tightly as this will spoil the effect.

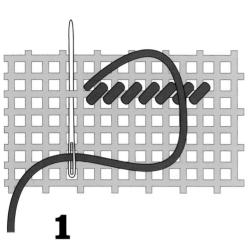

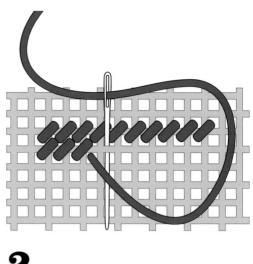

The most basic tapestry stitch is a
half cross stitch and is suitable for
most projects.

tip:

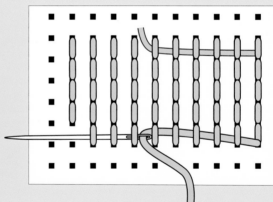

When starting a new length of thread hold the end
of the thread at the back of the work and sew the
first few stitches over it to prevent the stitches
from coming undone. When finishing a thread pass
the ends through the backs of the stitches to keep
everything neat. Use the same method for both
cross stitch and tapestry.

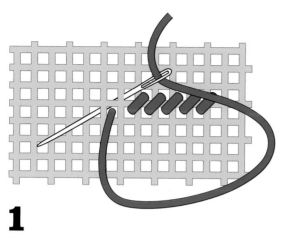

1

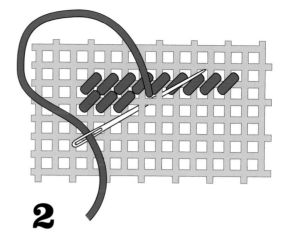

2

However, on canvas which has large holes the canvas may show through in which case tent stitch (see above) is best. This gives a denser finish but it does require quite a lot more wool.

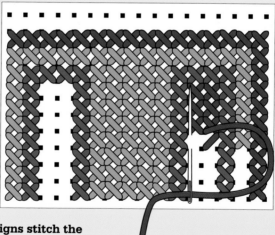

In more complicated designs stitch the outlines first followed by large areas of a single colour. Fill in the small areas of other colours last.

Project: 20 Stitch a sampler

These designs offer an alternative, contemporary take on the traditional sampler. Make up your own designs featuring your own home and personal possessions. It is not necessary to fill in all of the background – in many old samplers the motifs are stitched in outline with the background left unstitched. However, they look more finished if you do some filling-in and even better if the whole lot is stitched. In these designs the white areas can be left blank or stitched in white or if you prefer, a bright, contrasting colour.

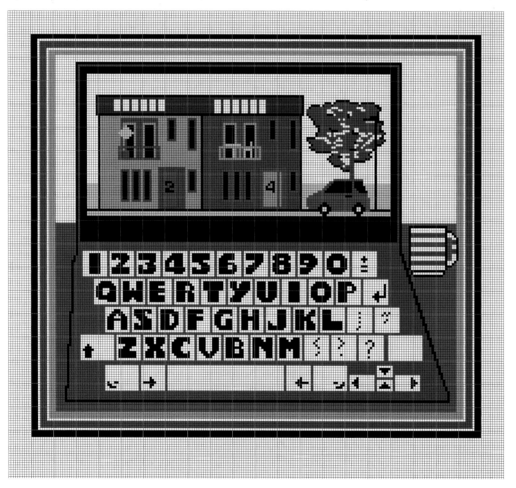

This sampler is 200 x 173 stitches. Depending on which count fabric you use, the finished size of the sampler will vary. If you use an 11 count cross-stitch fabric the sampler will be quite large approx 46 x 41 cm (18 x 16 in). Using an 18 count fabric will produce a smaller, finer piece of work measuring approx 28 x 24 cm (11 x 9½ in).

This smaller design is more suited to a larger hole cloth.
It is 96 x 117 stitches and made on an 11 count fabric
will measure approx 23 x 30 cm (9 x 11½ in) and with
the larger 6 count fabric will measure approx 41 x 51 cm
(16 x 20 in).

Project: 21
Make a sketch book cover

Use a piece of your cross stitch to decorate a sketch book cover. The measurements given here are for a cover for an A5 (5¾ x 8¼ in) sketch book.

For a finished cover measuring approx 17 x 24 cm (6⅔ x 9½ in) and a pocket 16 x 20 cm (6¼ x 7¾ in) you need three pieces of fabric.
Cover: cut two pieces 20 x 51 cm (7¾ x 20 in).
Pocket: cut one piece 19 x 23 cm (7½ x 9 in).

Materials:
Choose a fabric which is quite stiff. An artist's canvas is ideal but you must pre-shrink it by washing it before using. Otherwise go for a thick cotton twill or chunky linen as used for upholstery. It doesn't have to be plain – ticking and other stripes would also work well.

1
Turn in the sides of the completed cross stitch and tack.

2
Machine or hand stitch the cross stitch on to one of the cover pieces leaving 3.5 cm (1⅓ in) at the bottom.

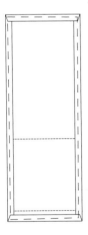

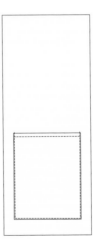

3
Snip the corners, turn in the edges and tack down.

4
Turn in the edges of the pocket and stitch along the top edge.

5
Position the pocket on to the backing piece leaving 3.5 cm (1⅓ in) at the bottom and sew in place.

6
Turn in the edges of the remaining cover piece so that it is slightly smaller than the front.

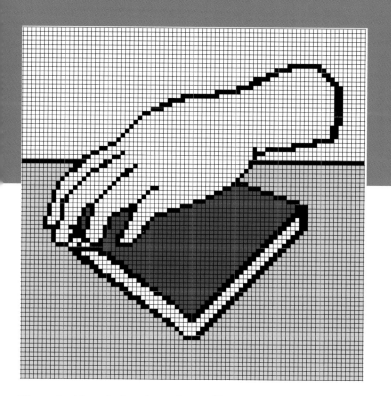

The embroidery design shown here will measure approx 14 cm (5½ in) square on a 14 count fabric.

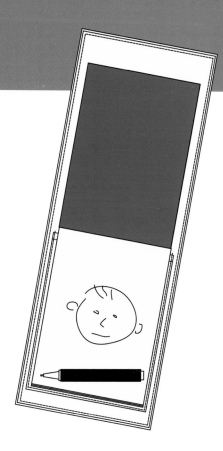

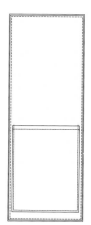

7

Tack the backing on to the front and attach by sewing along the edge of the backing piece.

8

Slide the card back of the sketch book into the pocket.

Project: 22 Make a tapestry bag

A good place to exhibit your tapestry skills is on a bag.

1

Trim the finished canvas leaving a 1.5 cm (¾ in) seam allowance all round. Choose a good thick cotton or canvas for the back of the bag and cut a piece the same size as the tapestry.

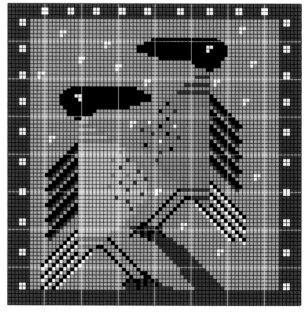

2

Turn over the top of the canvas at the top of the tapestry and with right sides facing machine stitch the two pieces together making sure that the line of stitching is along the edge of the embroidery. Turn over the top of the backing piece to match the front, turn right side out and press lightly.

3

To make the lining: cut two pieces of fabric slightly smaller than those used for the main bag and stitch along the sides and bottom, leaving the top edge open.

4

Press open the seams and turn over the top so that when it is inserted in the bag the top edge is slightly lower than the top inside the bag.

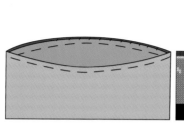

5

Tack the lining around the top of the the bag and oversew into place.

6

Make a handle (see page 42) and stitch firmly into position.

Project: 23 Stitch a portrait

These portraits were inspired by an Art Deco drawing and the fact that the original drawing is quite stylised made it easier to translate into charts.

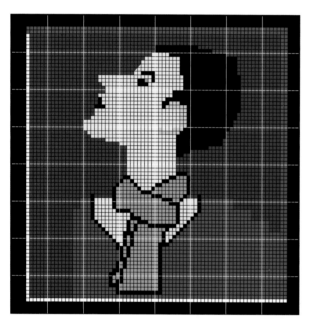

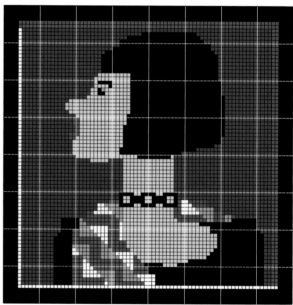

Frame it

When you plan your project leave a generous amount of canvas or fabric around the edges so that you can mount your needlework onto card ready for framing.

1

Cut a piece of thick card to the size of the stitched area and place on the centre of the wrong side of the work.

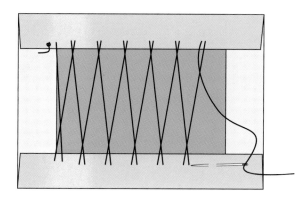

2

Fold over the top and bottom edge and thread lengths of strong thread through the two sides together as shown. When you reach the edge of the card gently pull the threads so that they are even and taut.

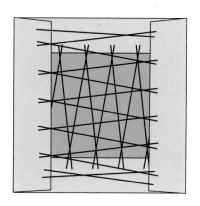

3

Fold over the remaining sides, folding in the corners. Stitch as before making sure that the edges are straight and the picture is central.

Project: 24 Stitch a self-portrait

Immortalise your own face in tapestry. It may not be an exact likeness but the results can be surprisingly convincing.

1

Choose a favourite photograph a side view is best as it creates the most distinctive shape.

2

Draw the silhouette onto tracing paper adding in obvious details such as eyes, eyebrows, jaw line and nose.

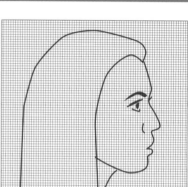

3

Transfer the line drawing on to squared paper. Use a thick pen as this will make it easier to work out the design.

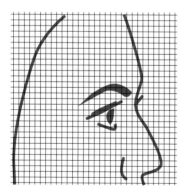

4

Start mapping the design following the line drawing.

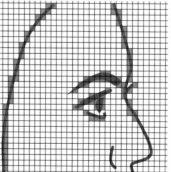

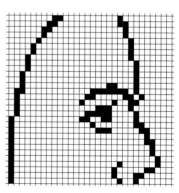

5

You won't be able to follow the lines exactly but a rough rule is to put a stitch in any square that the line runs through. Some adjustments will have to be made in order to make the design work so for the first draft use a pencil and fill in the squares lightly.

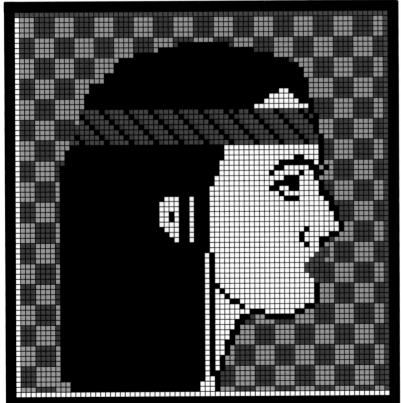

6 In this interpretation a hair band has been added for extra decorative interest. A patterned background is not essential but it makes it more interesting to stitch.

tip:

Use a handy computer programme to magically turn any image into a cross stitch or tapestry chart.

Project: 25
Small stuff

Just because you don't have time or patience for big stuff doesn't mean you can't show off your stitching skills. These small motifs can be used to cheer up a variety of objects, and keeping it small might inspire you to create your own designs even if it's just your name or initials.

Make a keyring

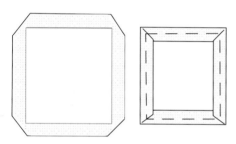

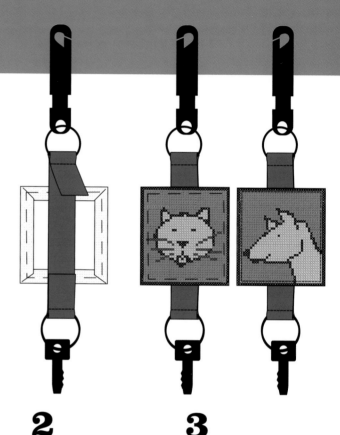

1

Sew two small embroidered motifs, trim the corners, turn in the edges and tack.

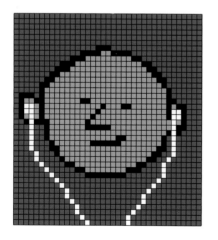

2

Stitch your keys and hook onto a piece of strong tape and place it centrally on the back of the first motif.

3

Place the second motif right side up on top and tack round the edges. Stitch all round the edge.

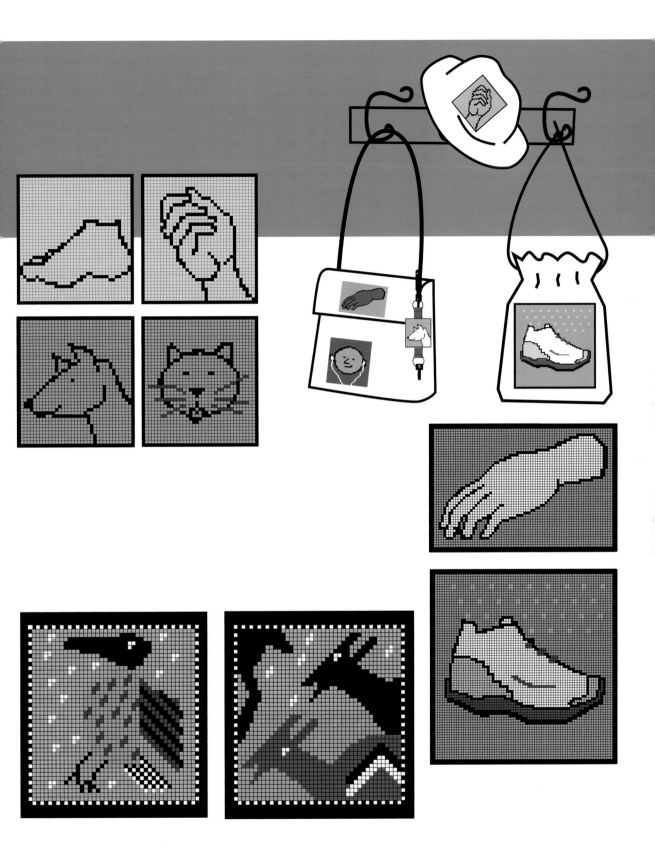

Accessories

Using the simple sewing techniques and your embroidery skills plus a few purchases from DIY stores and stationers it is possible to make some distinctive and quirky accessories.

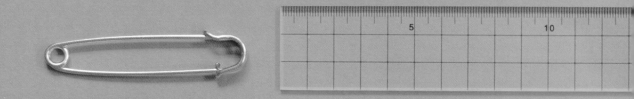

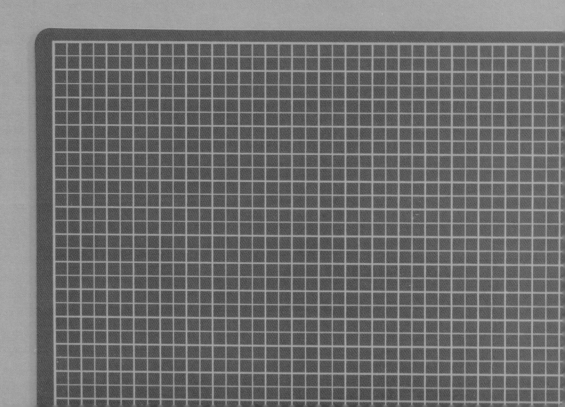

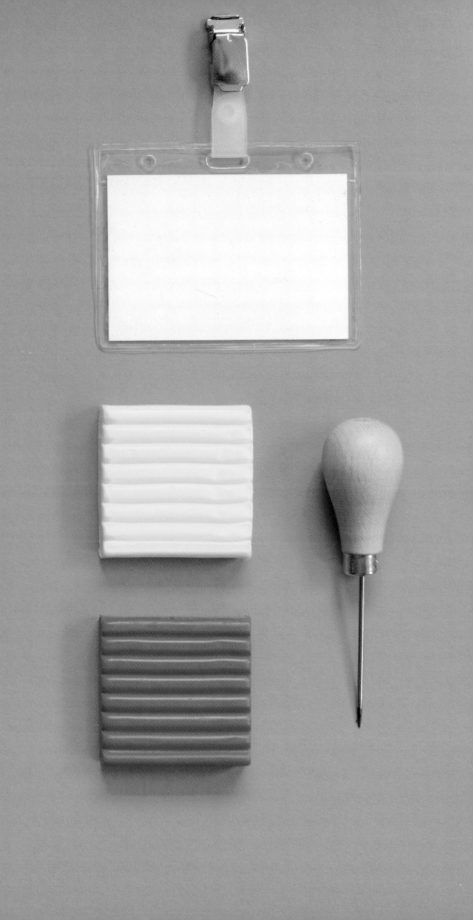

Hardware

Take a trip to the hardware store and stationers and be inspired to make your own jewellery.

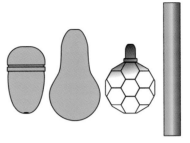

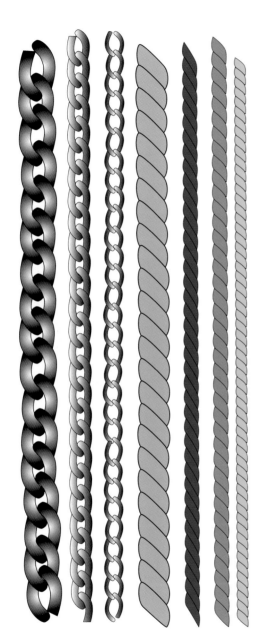

Light switch pulls come in a range of shapes and sizes. Materials include wood, coloured acrylics and ceramic.

Screw these 'eyes' in to wood or even plastic objects to turn them into pendants or charms.

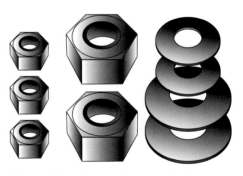

Nuts and washers make great beads.

Getting started Hardware and elements

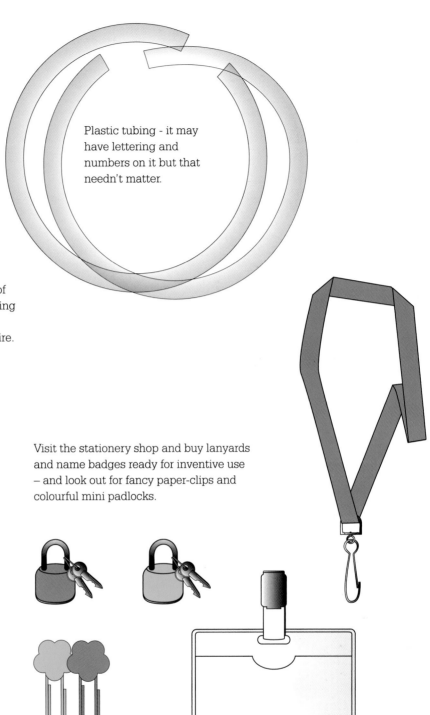

Plastic tubing - it may have lettering and numbers on it but that needn't matter.

Split rings come in a wide range of sizes and are very useful for hanging things from – much easier than fiddling around with pliers and wire.

Look in the kitchen departments for mini graters and whisks.

Visit the stationery shop and buy lanyards and name badges ready for inventive use – and look out for fancy paper-clips and colourful mini padlocks.

Project: 26
DIY jewels

You don't need any special tools to make these impressive jewels.

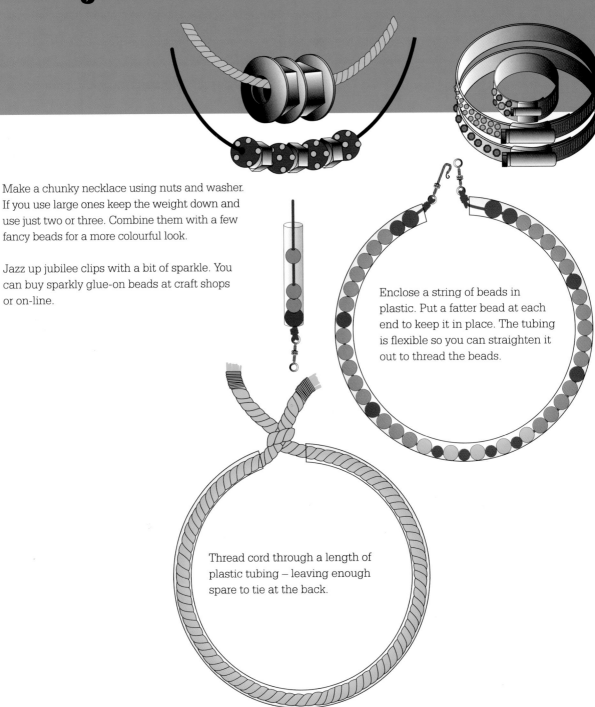

Make a chunky necklace using nuts and washer. If you use large ones keep the weight down and use just two or three. Combine them with a few fancy beads for a more colourful look.

Jazz up jubilee clips with a bit of sparkle. You can buy sparkly glue-on beads at craft shops or on-line.

Enclose a string of beads in plastic. Put a fatter bead at each end to keep it in place. The tubing is flexible so you can straighten it out to thread the beads.

Thread cord through a length of plastic tubing – leaving enough spare to tie at the back.

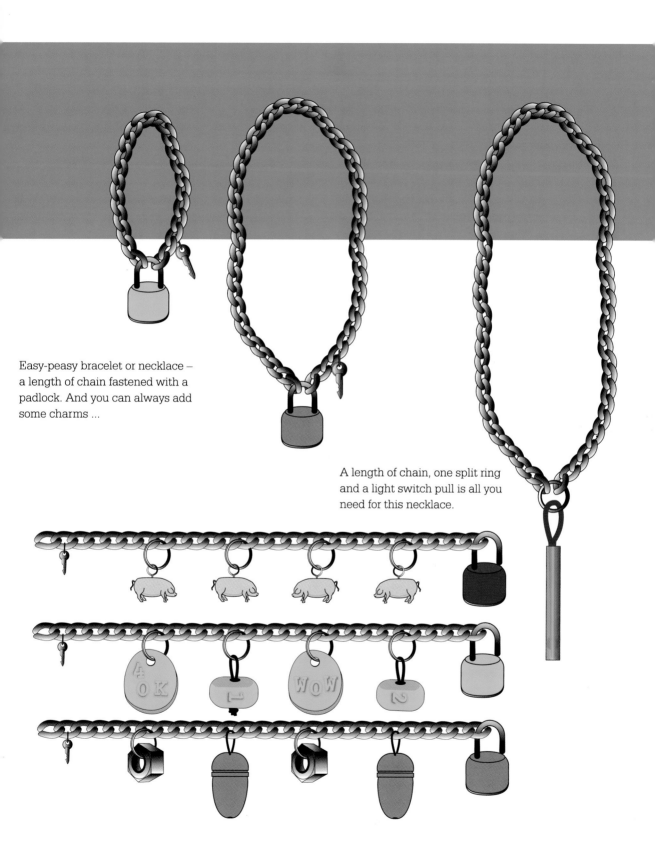

Easy-peasy bracelet or necklace – a length of chain fastened with a padlock. And you can always add some charms ...

A length of chain, one split ring and a light switch pull is all you need for this necklace.

Project: 27 Make some pendants

Pendants never go out of fashion and offer a great opportunity for ingenuity and inventiveness. There is really no limit to what you can hang from them be it your artwork, memento, lucky find or even some kitchen utensils.

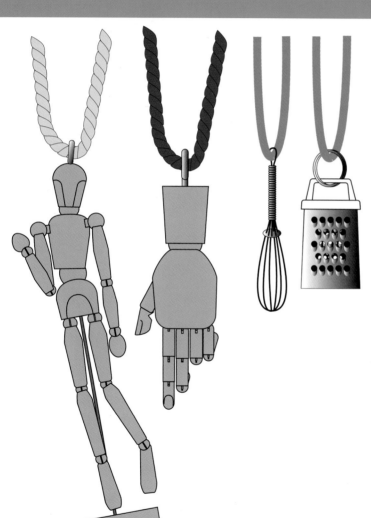

Screw eyelets into small versions of the artist's figure and hand and hang them from rope or cord. Mini cooking utensils not only make fun pendants, but are also handy for culinary emergencies.

Make some earrings

If you are careful you can screw small eyes into plastic farm animals to make piggy earrings.

Paint a small wooden light switch pull, attach it to the earring with a loop of thick thread or thin cord.

Thread a few fancy paper-clips onto a split ring.

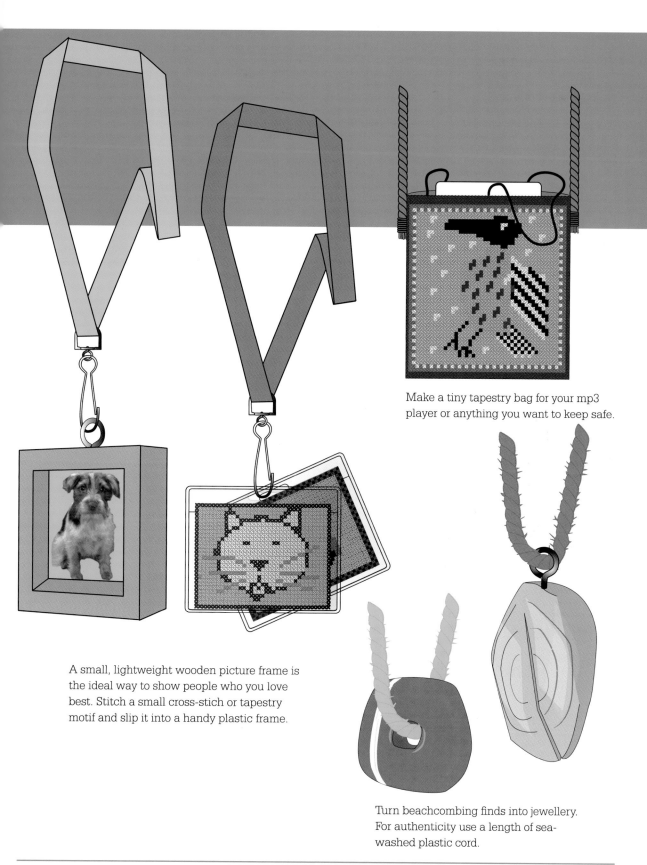

Make a tiny tapestry bag for your mp3 player or anything you want to keep safe.

A small, lightweight wooden picture frame is the ideal way to show people who you love best. Stitch a small cross-stich or tapestry motif and slip it into a handy plastic frame.

Turn beachcombing finds into jewellery. For authenticity use a length of sea-washed plastic cord.

Project: 28
Re-invent
old jewellery

If you haven't got odd bits of jewellery in need of re-invention then you can find other people's cast-offs in charity shops (or older relatives' jewel boxes). It is easy to create stunning pieces using the traditional kilt pin. You can buy them plain or get special ones with loops from craft shops or from internet suppliers. These offer a great way to use those single earrings you couldn't bear to throw away when you lost its partner, and an opportunity to wear much-loved pieces in a new way.

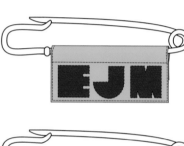

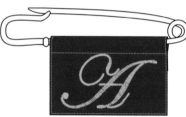

Embroider a smart monogram using appliqué or satin stitch.

tip:

Pieces will work best if you use items of similar theme or colour.

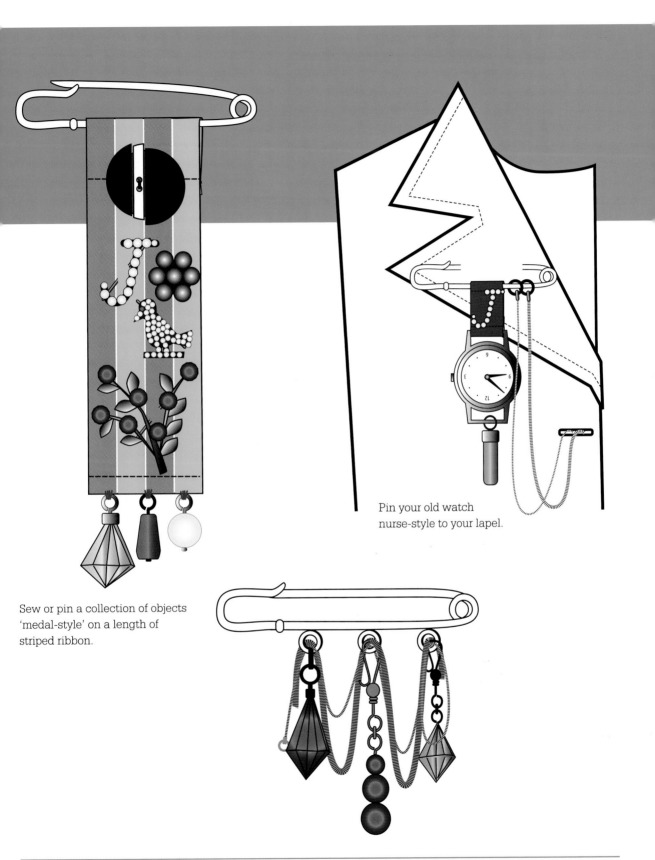

Sew or pin a collection of objects
'medal-style' on a length of
striped ribbon.

Pin your old watch
nurse-style to your lapel.

Make it, stamp it, bake it

Modelling clays designed to be hardened in the oven are available in a range of colours and can be used to create a wide variety of beads, buttons and charms. There are lots of commercial kits, moulds and designs but they can be complicated to make. It is much better to make something simple and personal. The designs here are very easy to construct as they avoid sharp edges and regular shapes. When buying the materials go for the 'soft' versions as they are easier to work with.

Getting exact, crisp shapes requires skill, patience and sometimes extra equipment but a simpler, less precise shape is not only easier to do but gives a more interesting, less commercial look.

A set of rubber stamp letters intended for printing is ideal for putting your own stamp on modelling clays. Use them for names, initials and messages.

1
Take a lump of modelling material and roll it in your palms to form a ball.

2
Use a rolling pin to flatten it slightly and form a shape that is rounded but flat on the top and bottom.

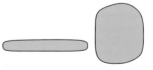

3
This shape is ideal for beads. Flatten it further and it is a good shape for buttons, charms and dog-tags.

Getting started Modelling clay

tip:

With these materials it is best to keep things simple otherwise they can look tacky. Stick to one colour and decorate boldly but simply.

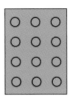

Textural impressions

Create textures with items such as cord and children's building bricks.

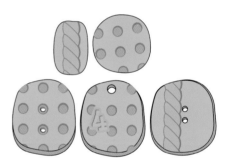

Roll out little balls in the same colour, press them on gently for a bobbly effect, press them more firmly for a more subtle texture.

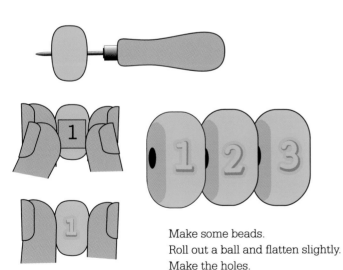

Make some beads.
Roll out a ball and flatten slightly.
Make the holes.
Decorate to taste.

tip:

Make the holes with a sharp pointed tool such as a bradawl. The hole on the back will be a bit ragged so push the bradawl in from both sides gently wriggling it around to smooth the edges of the hole.

Project: 29 Make some buttons

Make a ball as before and roll out to a thickness of approximately 0.5 cm (¼ in) (make them thicker if you wish), the shape will not be symmetrical but that's OK.

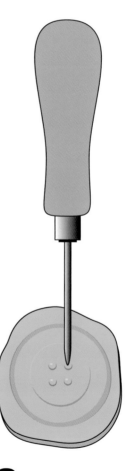

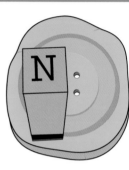

When you press the buttons into the clay the holes form raised bobbles so turn these into part of the design and put the holes elsewhere.

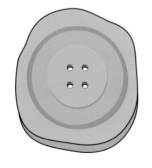

1
Choose a button, preferably one that is not too flat and press it firmly into the modelling material.

2
Carefully peel the clay from the button and gently press flat.

3
Make the holes using the impression as a guide.

4
Apply lettering or numbers using a set of rubber stamps.

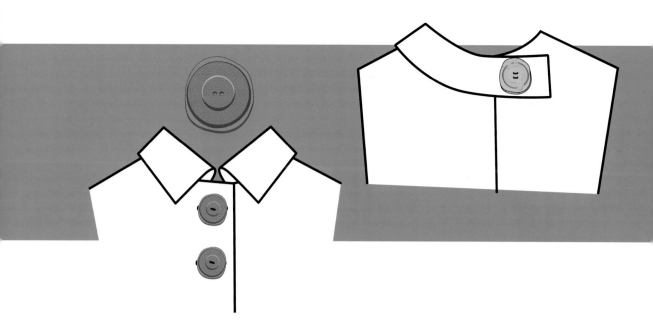

1

Roll out a piece of modelling clay and bend it carefully over a knitting needle or bradawl.

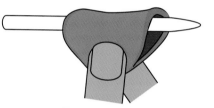

2

Pinch the ends together.

3

Make a hole.

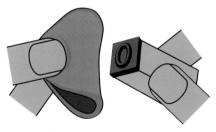

4

Hold firmly between finger and thumb and stamp in the letter.

5

Use as a button or tie together with cord and make some cufflinks.

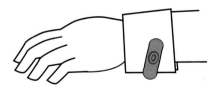

Project: 30
Sew some jewellery

Patchwork

Cut a piece of backing fabric allowing for turning all round. Cut a piece of stiffening fabric the size of the finished piece of patchwork (use a stiffener such as buckram available from sewing /craft stores or online), place it on the backing and fold the edges in over it. Tack in place.

Stitch the two pieces together.

For the necklace insert an eyelet at the top and hang from thick cord with a split ring.

For the brooch omit the eyelet and stitch a pin on the back.

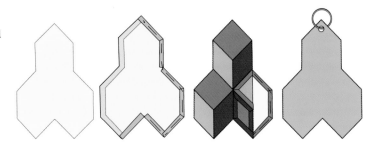

Knitting

Knit lots of skinny strands (see page 31) and twist them together. Knitting is stretchy so no need for fastenings, just pull them over your head or over your hand.

Make a hair ornament by stitching together the strands and attaching them to a hair slide.

Make a bracelet by stitching the patchwork to a piece of fabric or wide ribbon and tie with more ribbon.

Quilting

The vegetables featured in the quilting chapter can be adapted to make quirky jewellery. You can sew the pieces together using blanket stitch or oversewing.

  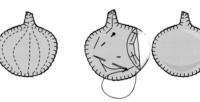

1

Cut out a front and back (allowing for a turning allowance all round) and a piece of wadding slightly smaller than the finished shape.

2

Turn in and tack. Blanket stitch or oversew the two pieces together. Add extra stitching as shown.

3

For a slightly fatter look use filling instead of wadding and miss out the extra stitching.

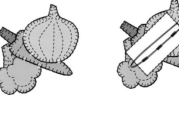

Make a brooch

Stitch the vegetables together on the back making sure the stitches don't show on the front.

Stitch a stiffish piece of fabric to the back and stitch on a large pin. Alternatively stitch them on to a hair slide or comb to make a hair ornament.

Project: 31
Sew a locket

A new take on the locket. Why not carry photos of your loved ones (or ancestors) in a tiny quilted book?

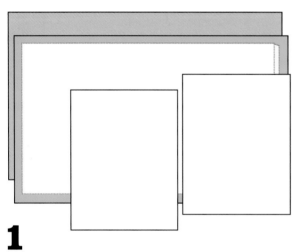

1

Scan in the photographs, print transfers (see page 148) and fix the image on to rectangles of white or off-white fabric.

2

Stitch the 'portraits' onto the backing fabric (as it is so small it is easier to do this by hand) positioning them so that there is enough space for the stitching around the edges and down the middle.

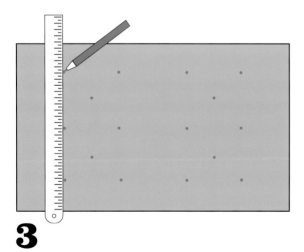

3

Work out and mark the position of the quilting stitches leaving enough fabric at the edges and middle for sewing up.

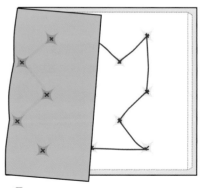

4

Pin or tack the fabric to the wadding and quilt using small crossed stitches.

5

Place the front and back together with right sides facing and stitch around the edge avoiding the wadding and leaving a gap for turning right side out as (see page 71).

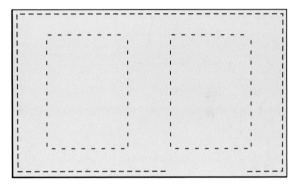

6

Turn right side out and sew up gap.

7

Fold in half and stitch along the fold far enough from the edge for a cord to be threaded through. Sew on cord or ribbon ties (you can omit these if you wish).

8

To wear, thread cord through the spine.

Project: 32
Make a
photo wallet

A larger form of the locket and made in the same way as the cross stitch note pad on page 84, this wallet is another way to carry special pictures around. Pop it in your bag or hang it on a cord as a pendant.

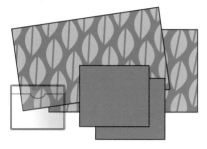

1

For a finished size of approximately 9 x 11 cm (3½ x 4⅓ in) when folded Cut two pieces of fabric 13 x 26cm (5 x 10¼ in) for the main wallet. Cut two pieces of fabric 13 x 11cm (5 x 4⅓ in) for the pockets. One plastic name badge holder. Length of ribbon.

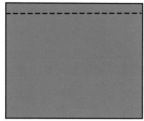

2

Turn in the edges of the pocket and stitch along the top edge.

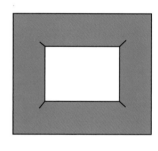

3

Cut a hole in the centre of the other pocket piece, snip the corners.

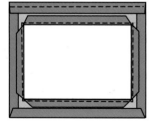

4

Turn in all the edges. Stitch around the inner edge of the hole and along the top of the pocket.

5

Turn in the edges of both large pieces.

6

Tack the pockets into position and stitch around the three sides of each one leaving the top open.

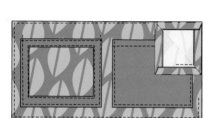

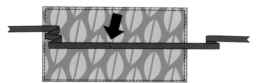

7

Place the pieces wrong sides
together and stitch around the edge.

8

Secure the ribbon tie with a few
stitches on the fold line as above.

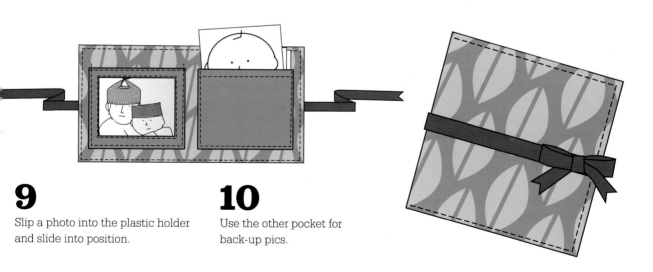

9

Slip a photo into the plastic holder
and slide into position.

10

Use the other pocket for
back-up pics.

Project: 33
Cheer up
an old belt

Rejuvenate an old belt by covering it with a piece of your needlework.

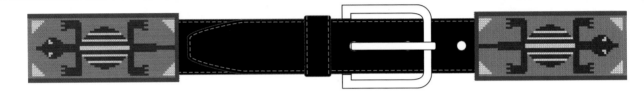

Decide on which belt you wish to use and stitch a length of tapestry long enough to cover most of the belt but leaving enough room for fastening the buckle. It should be wide enough for the belt to slot through, but narrow enough so that it fits quite snugly. Don't forget to leave enough canvas all round for turnings. Cut a piece of fabric for the backing allowing for turnings. When turned in this piece should be the same size as the turned-in piece of tapestry.

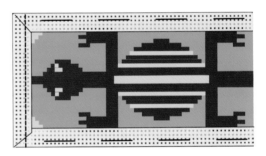

1

Turn in the edges of the piece of tapestry along the stitched edge and tack down. Stitch along the end edges.

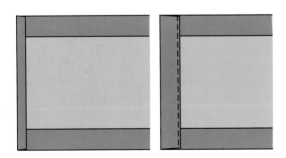

2

Turn in the sides of the fabric piece, turn over both ends twice as for a hem, and stitch down along the end edges.

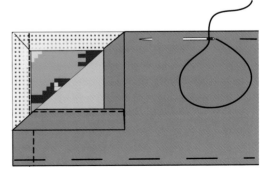

3

Tack the backing fabric on to the tapestry. Stitch along the long sides leaving the ends open.

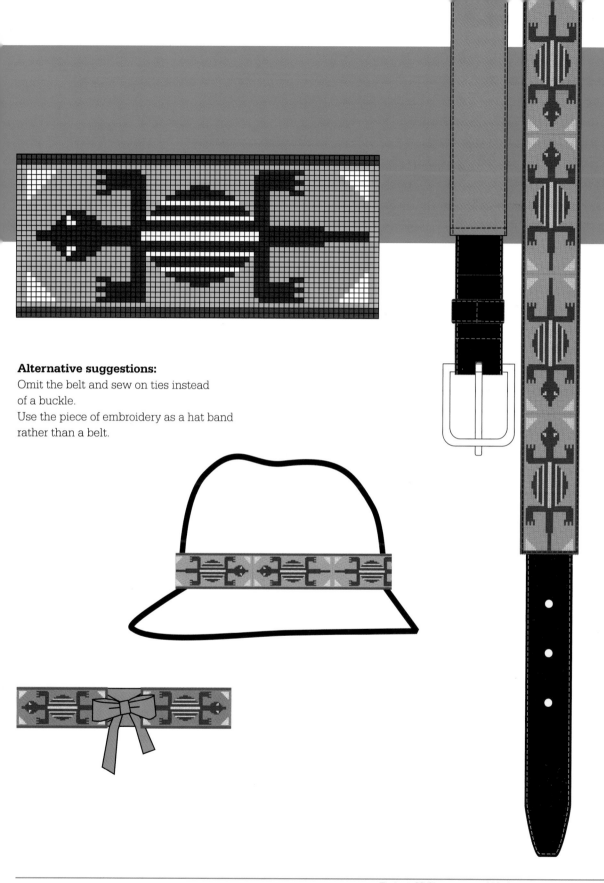

Alternative suggestions:

Omit the belt and sew on ties instead
of a buckle.

Use the piece of embroidery as a hat band
rather than a belt.

Project: 34 Re-use and re-cycle

Your jeans may be worn out but the pockets usually survive and can be put to good use.

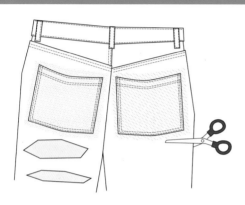

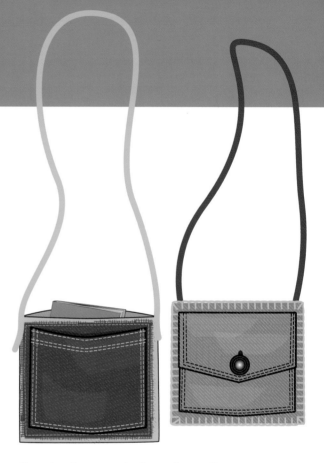

Sew a pocket on to the front of a small shoulder bag.
Use a jacket pocket with a flap and button – blanket stitch round the edge to stop it fraying.

Sew ready-made pockets cut from a pair of jeans or denim jacket onto a tote bag.

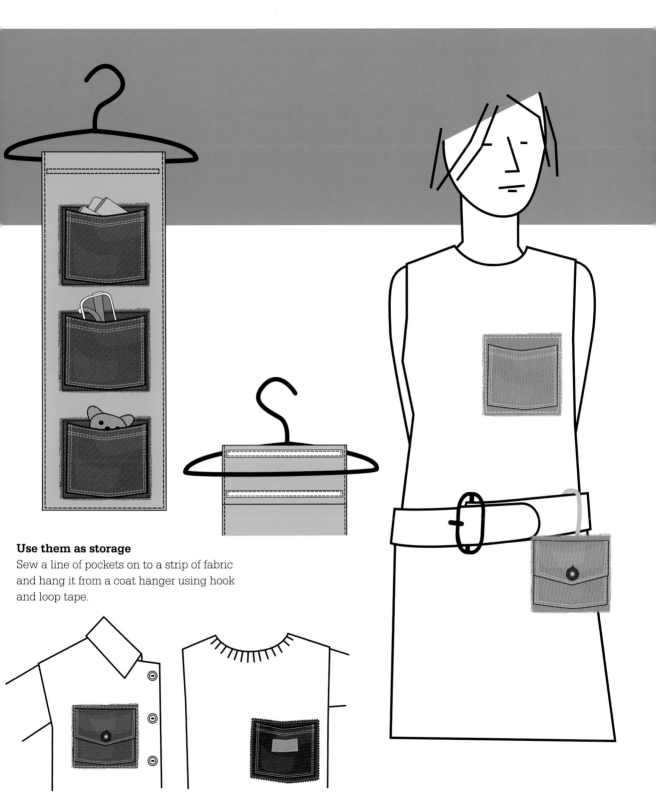

Use them as storage
Sew a line of pockets on to a strip of fabric
and hang it from a coat hanger using hook
and loop tape.

Re-invent an old shirt or jumper
by adding a pocket.

Paper

Take paper, card and art materials, add some computer technology and a dash of artistic skill to produce a range of items from photo frames to great art.

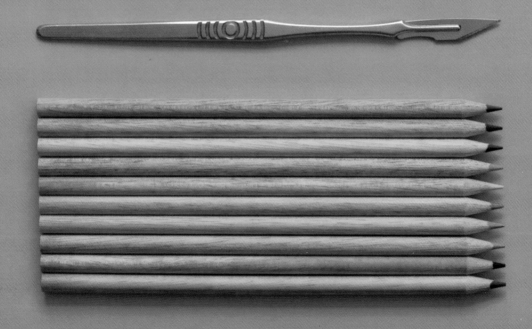

Paper Tips

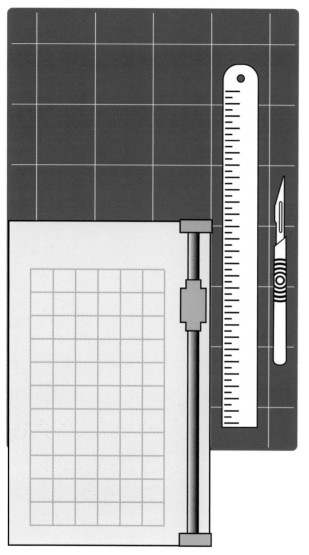

Useful equipment:

Cutting board: safer for you and the furniture.
Metal ruler: for measuring and cutting straight lines.
Scalpel or craft knife with renewable blades: essential for a clean cut. Blades with a long point are useful for intricate cutting out.
Paper cutter: not essential but good for straight edges and some have folding devices.

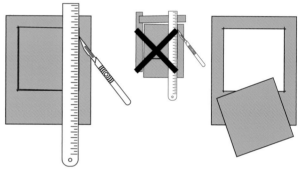

Cutting tips:

When cutting out a shape leave the surrounding paper or card intact. This prevents inaccuracies and mis-alignment.

Intricate shapes:

Straight cuts are easier than going around curves so for intricate shapes make a series of straight cuts rather than trying to cut around every nook and cranny.

Getting started   **Cutting**

*spray mount:
Useful stuff but use with
great care.
Read the instruction on
the tin before use.
Don't breathe in the spray
and wear a mask if you are
doing a lot of spraying.

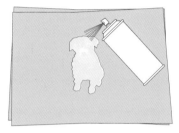

Don't use indoors:
Protect surrounding areas as the spray drifts.
Place items to be sprayed on several sheets of
newspaper.

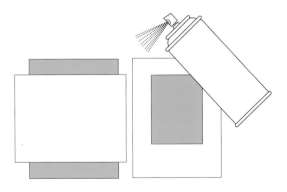

If you only need to spray a specific area use
clean paper to mask the area.
Once you have positioned the glued shape,
place a clean sheet of paper on top and use
your hand to smooth it down and eliminate
any air bubbles.

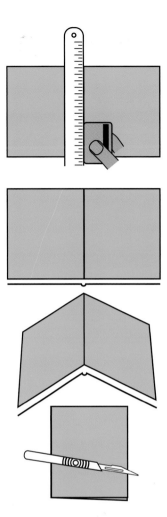

Folding paper:
Paper folds more easily and neatly
if it is scored first. Use an old credit
card or a blunt, non-serrated knife
to score a line on top of the fold.
Ease it carefully using both hands.
Flatten the edge by running a
smooth tool such as a scalpel handle
along the fold.

Spraying, folding

Project: 35
Folding books: record your adventure

Instead of filing your holiday pictures away print them out and make a journal. Folding books are ideal for this as they are easy to make and can be displayed in a variety of ways.

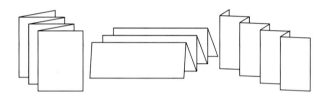

The size and shape of folded books is up to you, but it is easier to stick to proportions dictated by the paper size as this avoids too much cutting which can lead to inaccuracies. Stiff cartridge paper is better than card as it folds more easily. The folds don't have to be at regular intervals and can even be random to fit in with your images or design. Tiny versions are charming though you may need to use a lighter weight paper.

Sticking pictures in an album can be boring so turn your holiday into a comic strip complete with speech bubble commentary. Use pictures of different sizes and crop in to provide variety including close-ups.
Don't forget you can use both sides to continue the drama.

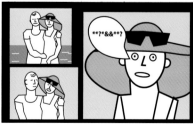

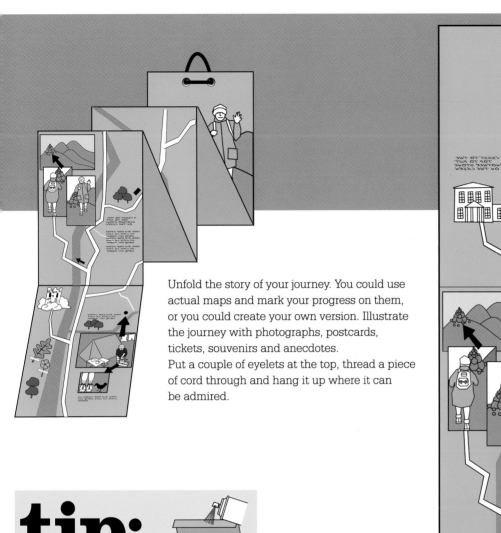

Unfold the story of your journey. You could use actual maps and mark your progress on them, or you could create your own version. Illustrate the journey with photographs, postcards, tickets, souvenirs and anecdotes.

Put a couple of eyelets at the top, thread a piece of cord through and hang it up where it can be admired.

tip:

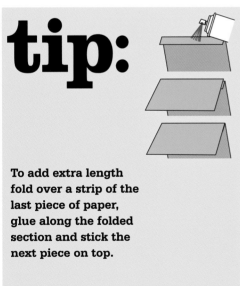

To add extra length fold over a strip of the last piece of paper, glue along the folded section and stick the next piece on top.

Project: 36
Record your life

Diaries are great but writing them can be a chore so why not create a snapshot of just one week of your life? It can be just once a year, but one week every season would give the bigger picture. The mundane often turns out to be the most interesting so take pictures of meals you have eaten (and the washing up), journeys to work,

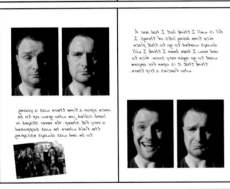

Take advantage of the huge choice of stylish notebooks available for your diary-keeping. Plain ones can be customised using your creative skills – anything from pictures and decoupage to designs using drawings or potato cuts. Alternatively you can assemble the pages and get them spiral bound at the local high-street printers.

The size and shape is up to you.

a week in the life

supermarket shopping trips and photographs of a typical evening watching TV or listening to music (together with details of what you were watching or listening to). Assemble layouts either on your computer or as a collage (or a mixture of both).

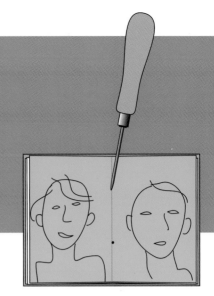

Portrait gallery

Why not draw the people who have played a role in your week? Even if you don't rate your drawing skills, portraits often turn out surprisingly insightful. If you want accuracy stick to photography, but remember that informality often gives a truer likeness than posed portraits. Children are brilliant at this so if you are too self-conscious let them do it for you.

Make a small book by sewing the pages together. If you have difficulty getting the needle through the paper make pilot holes using a bradawl. Use strong thread and tie the ends on the outside. This method works best with a small number of pages. Make the cover slightly bigger to stop the pages sticking out beyond it.

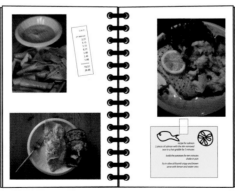

Keep a food diary

Hone your food photography skills and make a visual record of a week's consumption. Include recipes, shopping receipts and photos of any fellow diners.

Project: 37 Make a photo frame

Eyelet kits complete with metal hole punches are relatively inexpensive and can be used for a variety of craft projects.

Materials:
Two pieces of stiff card
A4 (8½ x 11 in) is a good size.
Eyelets and hole punch.
Cord (optional).

If you prefer free-standing frames attach a card stand to the back. Make your own stand (see page 131) or buy one ready-made from an artist's materials or craft supplies shop.

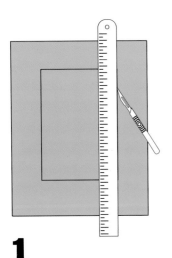

1

Cut out a rectangle leaving enough space around the edge for the eyelets.

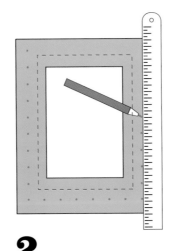

2

Measure and mark the position of the eyelets. Remember to leave enough space around the hole so that you can slide the picture (shown as a dotted line) into place.

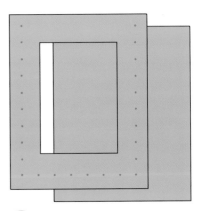

3

Place the front of the frame on the backing card.

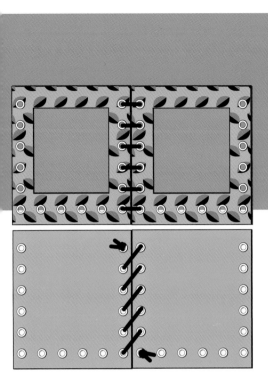

There are different ways to thread the cord
through, you could even tie two frames together.

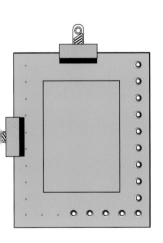

4

Hold them in place with bulldog
clips and put in the eyelets.

5

Slide the photograph into place.

6

Thread cord through the holes
and hang up (optional).

Project: 38 Make a lace-up book

Use eyelets to lace up your books to help keep your thoughts and sketches to yourself.

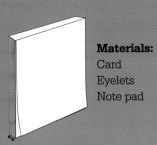

Materials:
Card
Eyelets
Note pad

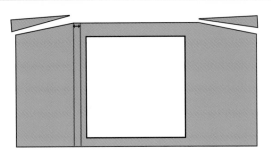

1

Cut a piece of card large enough to wrap around the note pad. When calculating the width, measure the depth of the note pad and add this measurement on both sides. Cut small triangles off each top corner as shown.

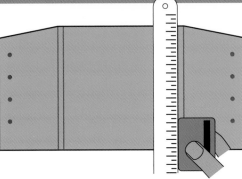

2

Mark the position of the eyelets. Score along the fold lines – don't forget to do this on the outside so that the score line is on top (see page 121).

3

Insert the eyelets. Spray adhesive on the back of the note pad and stick in place.

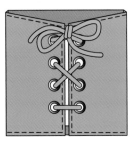

4

Lace up with coloured cord or a shoe lace.

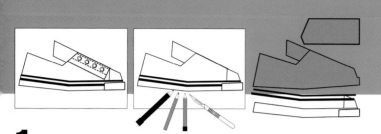

1

Trace or scan the sneaker minus the lace-up flap with eyelets on to paper (or directly onto the front book cover) and either colour-in or cut out the shapes from coloured card.

2

Make a separate piece for the lace-up flap adding a strip at the bottom for folding attaching.

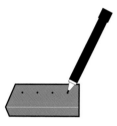
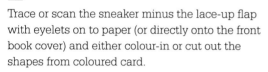

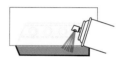

3

Mark the position of the eyelets on the lace-up flap.

4

Insert the eyelets and score along the fold line. Draw in the stitching.

5

Fold along score line then flatten out and spray adhesive on the folded strip.

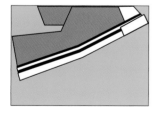

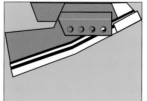
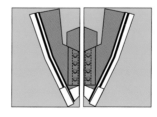

6

If you made the sneaker image separately stick it onto the front book cover.

7

Stick on the lace-up flap.

8

Repeat for the back cover remembering to make it a mirror image of the front.

9

Lace up with a lightweight cord as the flap may not be strong enough for anything too thick or heavy.

Project: 39
Make a 3D
family portrait

A different take on the family photo. Suitable for all partnerships, friendships and house-mates.

tip:

For a neater look use a photo manipulation programme to remove the backgrounds

1

Take photographs of your house, car (optional), the occupants and any pets.

2

Spray mount the house picture onto a piece of stiff card.

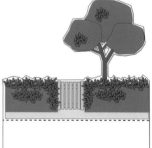 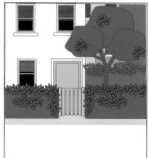

3

Spray mount another copy of the same view onto a piece of thinner card. Cut out as much of the background as possible leaving the foreground isolated with a strip of card at the bottom for folding.

4

Trim the pictures of the car, family and pets (you don't have to keep them in scale you can make the family, or the dog, bigger), spray mount them on to thin card and cut round removing as much of the background as possible. Leave a strip at the bottom for folding as in step 3.

7

Fold back the bases of the cut-outs and stick them down.

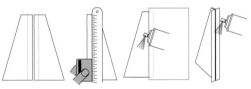

5

Cut a base from the thinner card, fold it and stick it to the back of the large background image. Choose a base colour to blend in with the scene.

6

To make a stand cut two pieces of card with a strip for folding along the straight edge. Score along the fold. Mask the folded strip and spray adhesive on the large area. Stick the two pieces together, fold out the 'wings', spray with adhesive and and stick down.
Alternatively, you can buy stands from artist's and craft materials suppliers.

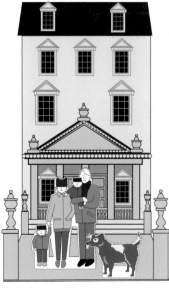

Of course, you don't have to stick to the truth.

Project: 40
Cut out doll

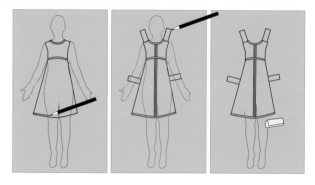

Take a picture of your friend / wife / partner / child, glue it on a piece of card and cut out. Leave a rectangle at the base which can be folded so that the doll will stand up.

And you don't have to stick to females – you could give your male partner a make-over.

Making the clothes.

Place the cut-out doll on the paper and draw a light pencil line around the shape which you can rub out before cutting out. Draw the clothes using the pencil line as a guide and colour/decorate as required. Work out where to put the tags and draw them in positioning them so that the fold is on a straight line. Make the tag long enough to hold the clothes in position and short enough so that it is not visible when folded.

Use coloured and patterned papers or create your own designs with pens, crayons or paint. Add details with stick on jewels, bits of fabric or feathers.

Project: 41
Do some decoupage

This is a drawing of a Decoupage picture
done in the 1850s. Ladies used to spend their
afternoons making pictures cutting out shapes
from paper and card and adding pieces of
fabric and rather charming paintings of their
pets. They also used shells, pieces of coral, tiny
tassels and miniature paintings. Decoupage is
often thought of as sticking small motifs onto
items such as lampshades, but this is more fun
and perhaps more often referred to as collage.

You could make a modern version reflecting your own tastes using contemporary furniture and featuring your own favourite objects. Use cuttings from furniture catalogues and magazines or draw your own. The blind can be made from strips of paper and the outside scene is up to you. And don't forget to add your favourite pet – use a photo or have a go at painting your own pet portrait.

Project: 42
Do some more decoupage

Apply your decoupage skills to your own home. Take a photo of your room – if possible with nothing in front of the window. Trace the shape of the window and cut out of paper or thin card. Do the same with furniture and any special features. Crop in the window view to put behind the frame. How you put everything together is

up to you. Using cut-outs, photographs, drawings and coloured and patterned papers you can reproduce what is there already or you could create fantasy rooms and furnishings – and by changing the view behind the window, move your home to a better location.

Project: 42
Make a
decoupage card

Freestyle style ...
Break free from reality and precision and give your creative talents free rein. Decoupage/collage is great for greetings cards. A good way to send friends your latest news – a wedding picture for instance, or the acquisition of a new pet.

Project: 43
Flick books

Materials:
Digital camera.
A5 (5¾ x 8¼ in) 160gsm card.
Scalpel / craft knife.
Straight edge.
Ruler.

The idea is to take a sequence of photographs which, when put together in a book, produce a moving image when 'flicked'.

Set the camera on continuous 'shooting mode' – sometimes called 'sports mode' or 'action mode' – keep the camera in one position (use tripod if you have one or lean on something to keep it steady). Take as many shots as the camera allows – some cameras can take up to 30.

The faster the shutter speed the more pictures you get so make sure the lighting is good.

For best results keep the subject matter simple and the backgrounds uncluttered.

If your camera can't do fast sequential shots just take a series of pictures – the movement will be more jerky but that can be more fun.

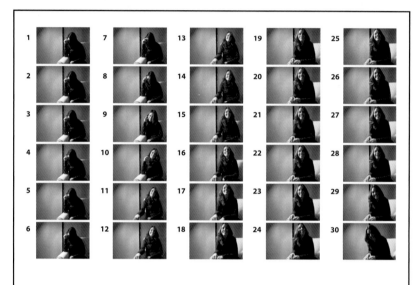

tip:

Print out a sheet of images in the correct order and number them, this will ensure you assemble them in the right sequence.

Import the pictures on to your PC.

Size the pictures so that three will fit on each sheet.

Using an A5 (5¾ x 8¼ in) set-up place the pictures onto the document making an allowance for the fact that the print area will be smaller than the document.

Print out.

Trim along the top, bottom and the right-hand edge.

Put them all together in order and secure them with a large bulldog clip.

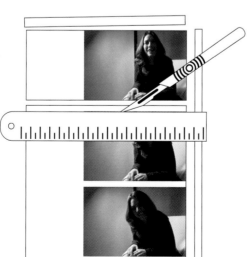

tip:

You can buy small notebooks which are ideal for flick books. Use them with photos or draw your own sequences.

Project: 44
Photo art

Turn your photos into art.

Blow your photographs up into big art. Scan at high resolution and divide up the image into A4 (8½ x 11 in) images (or whatever size your printer can manage). Mount them on thick paper or on thick card for something more permanent.

Design & Technology

Make the most of digital cameras, printers, computer programmes and the huge range of great craft materials to produce your own designs, prints and transfers.

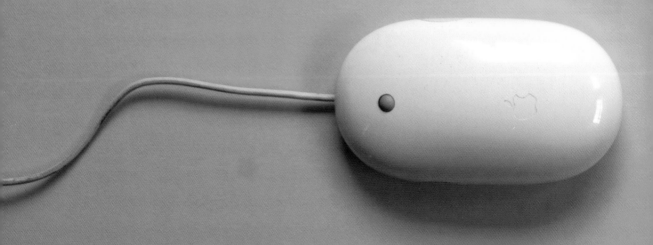

Scanning

With even the most basic computer programme you can scan images and adjust and manipulate them. You can crop, re-size, brighten, darken and re-colour, reflect and turn at any angle. Isolate parts of the image and use them with other photographs to make funny and surreal pictures.

Take one small picture of one small lamb, scan it, lose the background, import it with a transparent background and you can create a whole flock. If you are handy with photo or drawing programmes you can add colours and backgrounds to place people (and animals) in unexpected places.

Squeezing, squashing and turning things around can have quite creepy consequences.

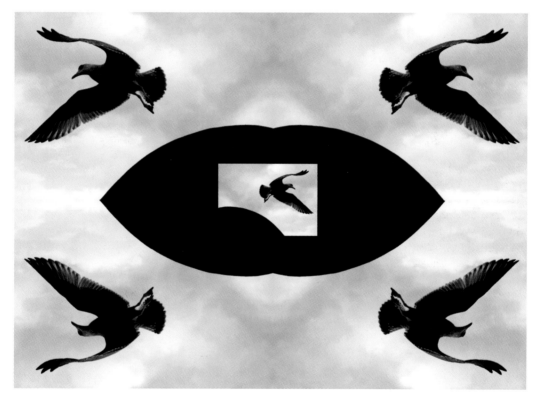

Take one photo, five copies and with a bit of
turn and turn-about you can create a striking,
unexpectedly dramatic image.

Project: 45 Make your own transfers

Great news for anyone wanting to print their own fabrics, t-shirts etc. is that you can now scan in an image and print it onto special paper which turns images into transfers that can be applied by ironing. Photos are obvious but use your imagination to combine different techniques and images.

Project: 46
Fun with fonts

Everyone has their favourite typeface but mostly use it in standard form with an occasional variation for headings or perhaps a letterhead. As well as allowing you to change the size even the simplest word processing and drawing programmes offer bold and italic versions of typefaces and the option of putting a line around the letters (referred to as stroke in the style options).

ABCDEFGHIJKLM
NOPQRSTUVWXYZ
1234567 8
abcdefghijklm
nopqrstuvwxyz

By adding an outline the letters take on a completely different character. Make this line very thick and they can become quite abstract while others develop strange points on the more angular letters. Experimenting with this can produce unusual and quite striking results, and if you have a programme that enables you to place images on top of one another in layers you can produce 3-D effects.

You might not have all of these typefaces but even the most commonly used ones can metamorphose into something unexpected.

These examples just use the stroke facility with no layers involved.

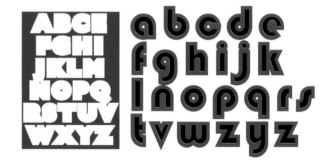

QWERTYUIOP
ASDFGHJKL;'
ZXCVBNM,.
ABCDEFG
1234567890
GH IJ
PQ
ABC

Build up a 3-D effect by combining layers with different line weights. Put the thickest on the bottom, reduce it for the upper layers and top it with the standard letters minus the outline. Varying the position can give an impression of movement or an interesting optical effect.

ZAP!
WOW! WOW! WOW!
WOW! WOW! WOW!
WOW! WOW! WOW!
POW!

Project: 47
Make your
own typeface

Why not invent your own typeface? Just draw it using pens, pencils and paper or use a mix of tracings, scans, cut-outs and scans. Import your creations on to your computer and use them in a photo or drawing programme. Use them in collage form on paper or put them together in computer-generated layouts.

These letters are easy to draw as they are formed from straight lines. Use graph paper and a ruler or draw them freehand for a looser look.

ABCDEFGHIJKLMNOPQRSTUVWXYZ

ABCDEFGHIJKLMNOPQRSTUVWXYZ

Create variations by varying the line weight or by filling in certain sections.

ABCDEFGHI
JKLMNOPQR
STUVWXYZ

This alphabet uses simple geometric shapes and despite being very stylised the letters are instantly recognisable and readable.

If you import your new typeface into a computer programme it can be squashed and stretched to give further variations.

ABCDEFG HIJKLMNOPQRSTUVWXYZ
ABCDEFG HIJKLMNOPQRSTUVWXYZ
ABCDEFG HIJKLMNOPQRSTUVWXYZ

By including a repeated regular element even the scruffiest handwriting can form a convincing typeface.

The repeat motif can be as simple as a coloured rectangle but you could also use a photograph. Alternatively, use a more complicated image reproduced using scanning and a computer programme.

By importing the letters as single images onto a drawing or image manipulation programme on your computer you can use them to create unusual headings, logos etc.

ABCDEFGHI
JKLMNOPQ
RSTUVWXYZ

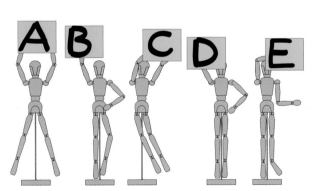

If you have a bendy man he can be used to hold up letters (attach them to the hands). If you want to be very ambitioius try putting him in positions that echo the letters. Photograph each one and assemble the alphabet on your computer.

Alternatively, draw the positions, or if all this seems just too much work stick to pin-men!

Project: 48 Draw your own fabric designs

Coloured fabric pens in a variety of thicknesses are great for drawing your own designs. Most are fixed using a hot iron – check the instructions to find out how best to use them. Choose from a variety of thicknesses to find one that suits your style. Freehand drawings have a certain charm and are best when kept simple. Opt for just one large drawing or use tracing paper to create a repeat design which can make even the crudest of drawings look sophisticated.

Keep it loose – don't try too hard and use long sweeping strokes for a more spontaneous look.

Create portraits by tracing over a photograph and give them a twist by using bold colours or drawing over a scribbled background.

If you are a confident artist go for a more painterly effect and use paint brushes and pots of fabric paints or inks, they are less easy to control but the results can be pleasingly arty.

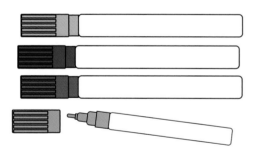

Project: 49
Print with potatoes

Potato cuts are not just for kids. It is possible to produce very grown up designs with simple shapes, good colours and a bit of imagination. Use them to decorate fabrics or paper. They are especially good for customising plain notebooks and cardboard boxes.

Use coloured inks that can be fixed. Do lots of practice prints before tackling the real thing.

1
Take a potato and wash it.

2
Cut it. Trim the skin round the top of the cut edge.

3
Draw on the design with felt tip pen.

4
Cut away the potato around the design.

5
Dab the potato on a piece of kitchen paper or a cloth to dry it off.

6
Apply the ink with a brush, sponge roller or by just dipping it into the ink.

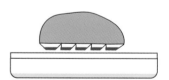

7
Avoid overloading the poato with ink as this will produce blurred, splodgy prints.

Project: 50 Stencils

Stencilling is often associated with fussy flowers and twee designs but if you stick to bold but simple shapes it can work well.

Draw the design on to a piece of card or paper. If you intend to do a lot of motifs a thick card will last longer but you can also use paper which is easier to cut.

Craft shops and websites offer a wide range of printing inks, some are gloopy while others are thin. Most are fixed with a hot iron but there are variations in fixing and application so read the instructions carefully before starting. Pour some colour into a plastic container and use a sponge to print. You could use a brush but spongeing produces better edges. Synthetic sponges are firmer and give a sharper image whereas natural sponges give a softer, less defined print. Sponge rollers give an even coverage but is not so suitable for use with thick card as it may not get into all the corners. Sponges produce a patchy, slightly uneven look which is part of the character. Practice on paper or spare fabric first as you need to work out amounts of ink and how hard to press as well as how often you need to re-load the sponge with more colour.

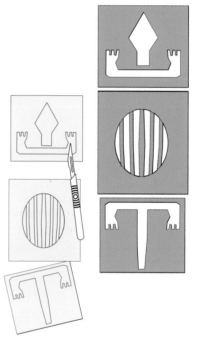

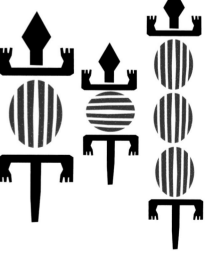

If you don't want to bother with cutting out card or paper just use the sponges to form the shape. Synthetic sponges can be cut into rectangles and triangles using a sharp scalpel or craft knife. Natural sponges give a nice blobby shape which will vary according to how hard you press or how much ink is on the sponge. A sponge ruler can be used for stripes.

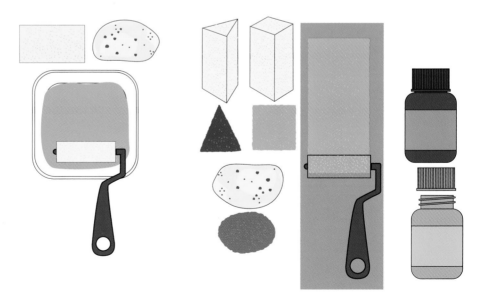

Templates

Templates and fonts are included for you to use but it is hoped that you will be inspired to create your own designs and patterns.

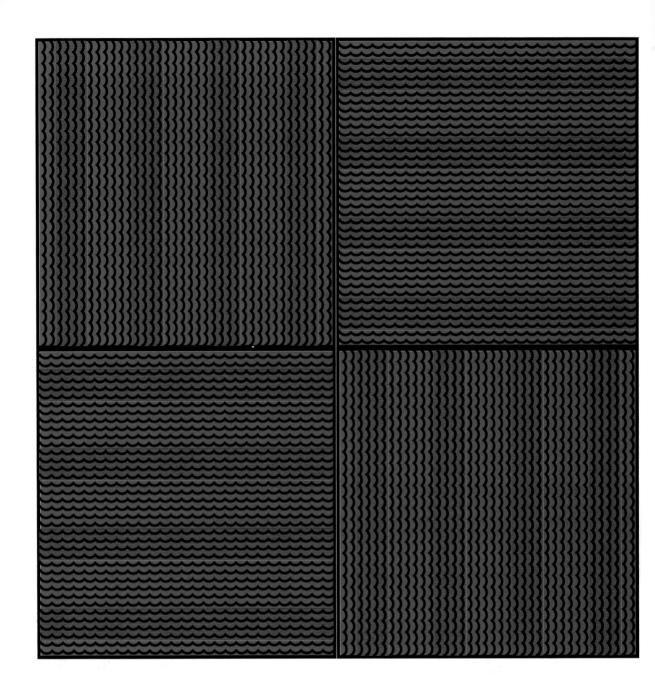

Knitted patterns

Fabric designs

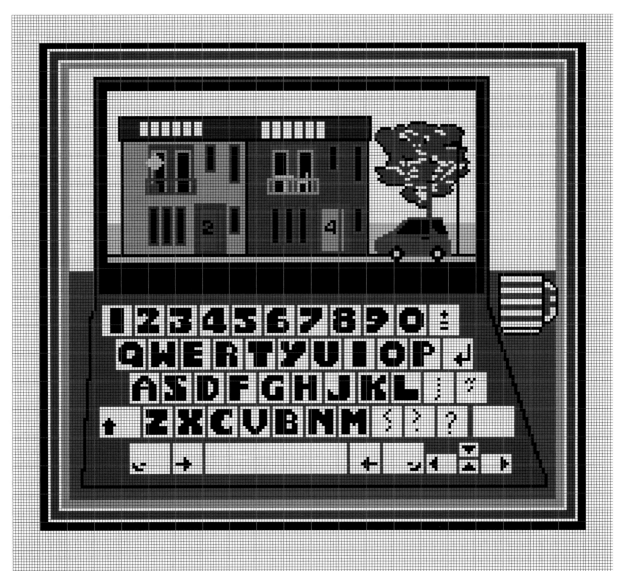

Samplers

Patterns

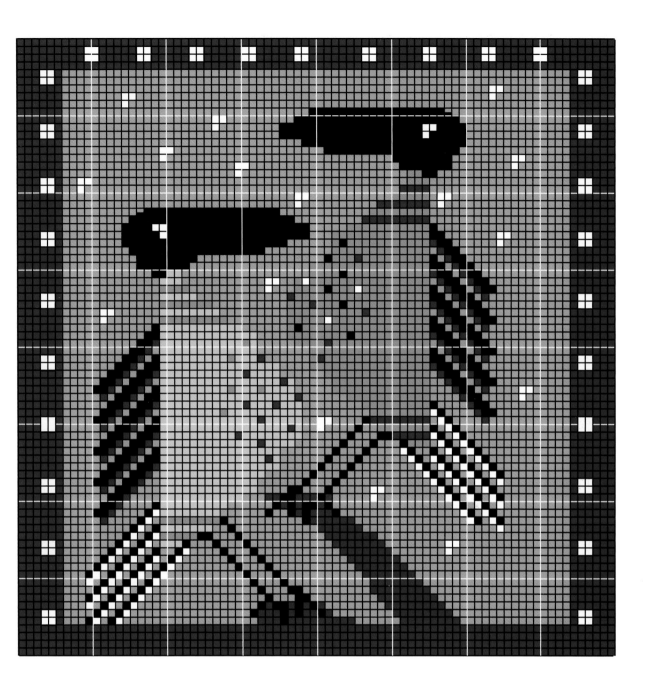

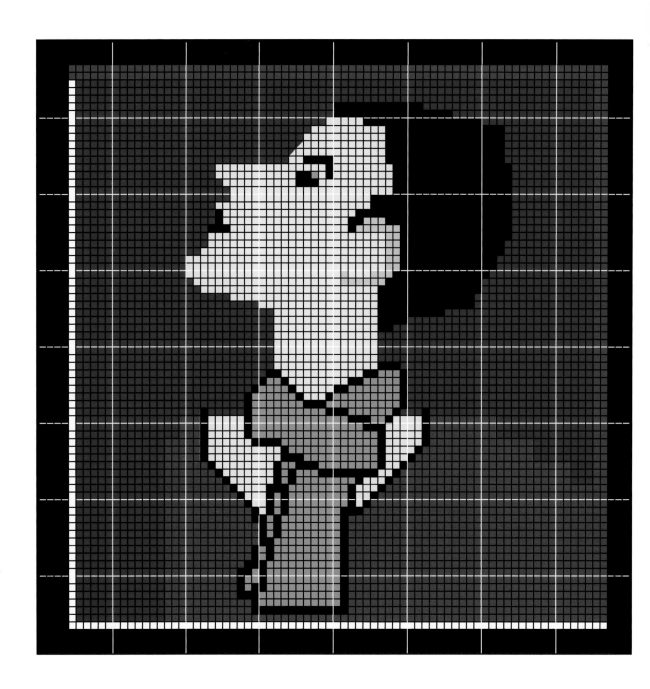

Cross stitch portraits

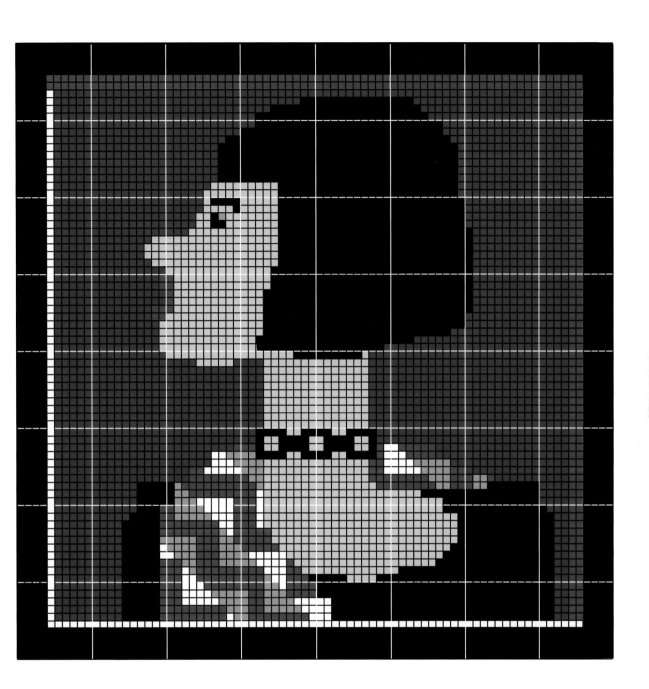

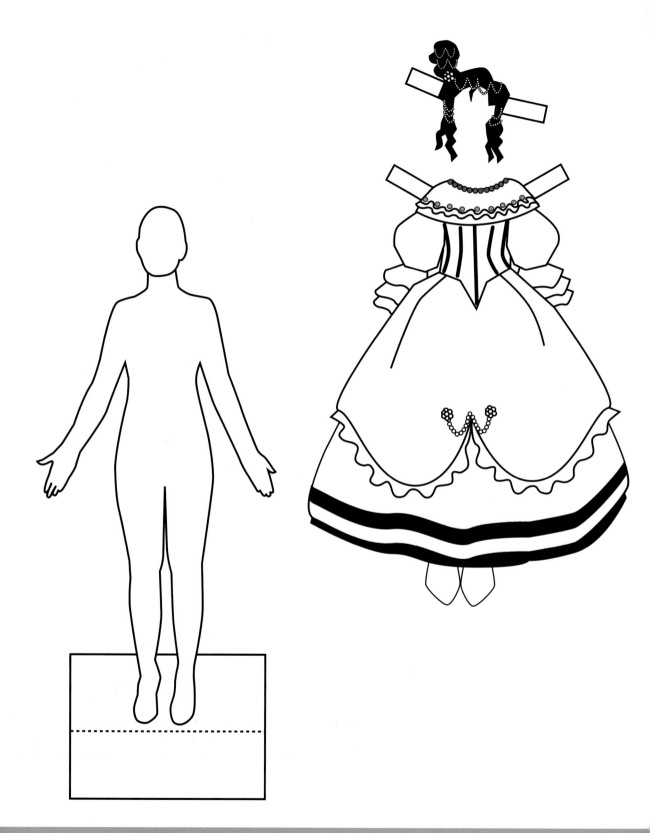

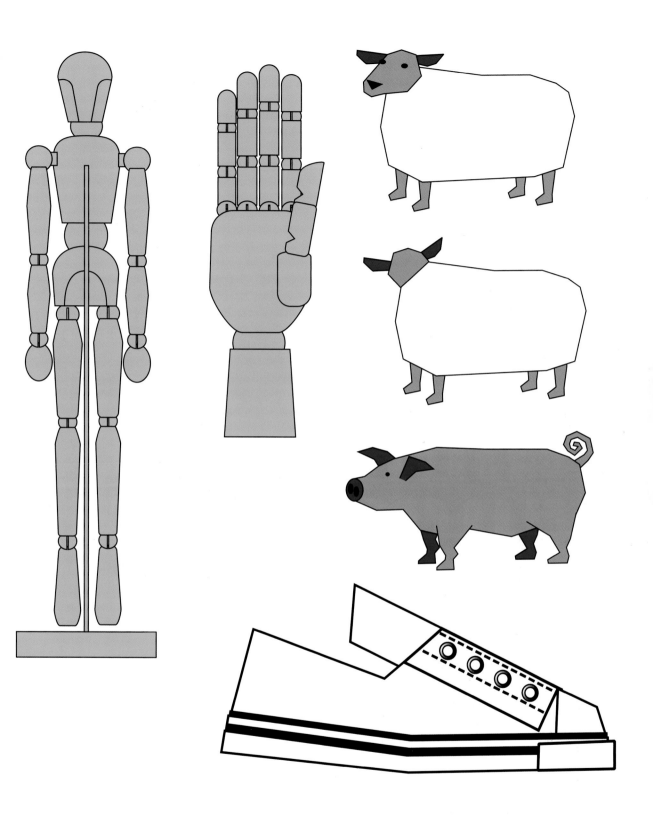

abcdefghi
jklmnopqr
stuvwxyz
0123456789

abcdefghi
jklmnopqr
stuvwxyz
0123456789

Typefaces

ABCDEFGHI
JKLMNOPQR
STUVWXYZ
0123456789

ABCDEFGHI
JKLMNOPQR
STUVWXYZ
0123456789

Many thanks to Roger Fawcett-Tang for the design and main photography and for his encouragement and use of colour.

Thank you to Lisa Pendreigh for using her editing skills and knowledge of craft to scrutinise the projects for inaccuracies and inconsistencies, and for all her helpful suggestions.

Thanks to Barney Bodoano for the additional photography, and for carrying out some very strange requests, and to Elizabeth Bodoano for being a willing model and not minding doing some odd things.

Thanks to William Bodoano and Steve Fuller for allowing me to raid their photograph albums.

Thank you to Vivays for commissioning the book and to Lee Ripley for her admirable patience in waiting for it to be completed.

Bridget Bodoano

Acknowledgements